City Slicker Wearside

Trevor Hopkins

A guide to sixteen mainly off road cycling routes for all abilities around Wearside and North East Durham.

Produced and published by City Slicker *Publications*
Fenham, Newcastle upon Tyne
telephone: 0191 273 6752
E-mail: trevor@cityslicker.demon.co.uk
URL: http://www.cityslicker.demon.co.uk

© City Slicker *Enterprises* 1997

First Edition 1997

British Library Cataloguing in Publication Data
A catalogue record for this book is
available from the British Library.

Text, Maps and Design by Trevor Hopkins

ISBN 0 9525593 2 3

Typeset and Printed by Sovereign Press, Felling, Gateshead

Contents

Location Map	4	Route 5. East Sunderland Circuit	21
Key to Symbols	4	Route 6. South Sunderland Circuit	25
Abbreviations	4	Route 7. Penshaw Circuit 1	31
Introduction	5	Route 8. Penshaw Circuit 2	35
Acknowledgements	5	Route 9. Hetton Lyons Park	39
City Slicker Guides	5	Route 10. Hetton Lyons Circuit 2	41
City Slicking	6	Route 11. Hetton Lyons Circuit 3	43
Types of Rights of Way	7	Route 12. Hetton Lyons Circuit 4	47
Maps	7	Route 13. Sacriston Circuit	51
Route 1. Sunderland Riverside 1	9	Route 14. Durham to Finchale	55
Route 2. Sunderland Riverside 2	13	Route 15. East Durham Circuit	57
Route 3. Sunderland Riverside 3	15	Route 16. Bowburn to Shincliffe	63
Route 4. Sunderland to Silksworth	19	Route 17. Cragside to No Place	65

Photographs

Front Cover: City Slickers on Wearside, Penshaw Monument (Route 8)
Photograph by Allan Glenwright

Rear Cover: By the 'Always Open Gates', St Peter's Riverside (Route 2)
Sculpture by Colin Wilbourn and Karl Fisher

Inside:

Timber Beach, Sunderland Enterprise Park	Route 1	page 11
Sunderland Riverside and Wearmouth Bridge	Route 3	page 17
Riding through Barnes Park	Route 5	page 23
'Two Plus Two' near Field House Farm	Route 6	page 27
Fording Burdon Dene	Route 6	page 29
After rain in Biddick Woods	Route 7	page 33
The ride out of Fatfield	Route 7	page 37
Passing Lilly Hill Plantation on Green Lane	Route 11	page 45
On the Mineral Line from Hetton to Low Moorsley	Route 12	page 49
At the top of Charlaw Lane	Route 13	page 53
Riding down into Cassop Vale	Route 15	page 59
View of Durham City near Old Durham	Route 15	page 61
'Journey's End' The Beamish Mary Inn, No Place	Route 17	page 65

Bikes, helmets and clothing for cover photographs supplied by:
Barrie Hopkirks Cycle Centre, 250 Shields Road, Byker, Newcastle upon Tyne
Denton Cycles, 21 Blenheim Street, Newcastle upon Tyne
'Primal Wear' clothing by **Jasun Direct,** telephone 01278 44711 for local dealers.

Location Map

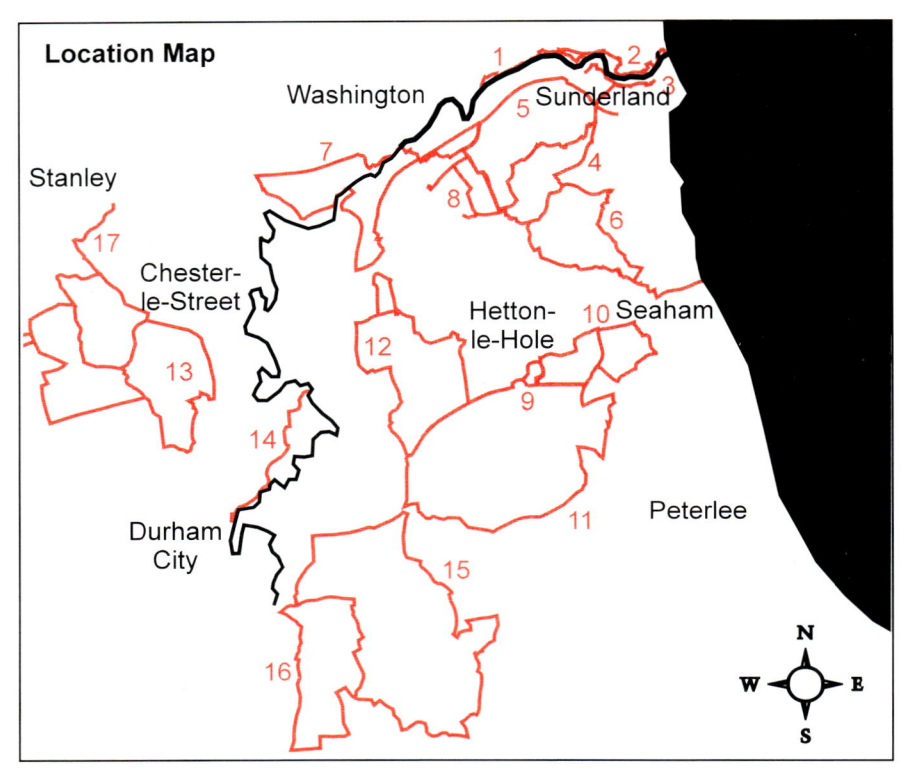

Washington
Sunderland
Stanley
Chester-le-Street
Hetton-le-Hole
Seaham
Durham City
Peterlee

Key to Symbols used on Route Maps

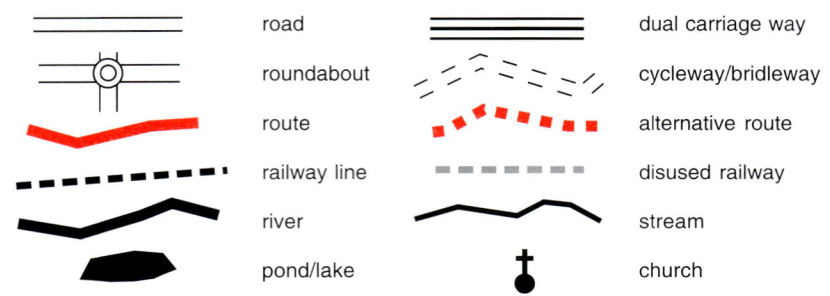

Symbol	Meaning	Symbol	Meaning
	road		dual carriage way
	roundabout		cycleway/bridleway
	route		alternative route
	railway line		disused railway
	river		stream
	pond/lake		church

Abbreviations used in Route Descriptions

TR	turn right	**(SO)**	straight on
TL	turn left	**(R)**	found on your right
R	right	**(L)**	found on your left
L	left	**(T) (M)**	trunk road/motorway

The routes and maps in this guide are no evidence of the existence of a right of way. The publishers cannot be held responsible for any omissions, accidents or injuries arising from following the routes suggested in this guide.

Introduction

After the success of my two guides for Tyneside I started to get a number of requests from cyclists and shops for a similar book for the Wearside area.

Now here I have to come clean and admit that I was born and have spent nearly all my life in Newcastle. Despite three years at college in Durham many years ago I knew very little about routes along the River Wear. I suspected that it would be difficult to find any good cycle routes in the area. How wrong I turned out to be! Durham County Council have, for some time, been building quality cycle routes across the county. Many of these are on disused railway lines. More recently Sunderland City Council has started to establish a network of routes connecting their urban and rural areas. In addition much of the area is covered by the Great North Forest, an organisation dedicated to improving both the quality of and access to the rural fringes of our urban areas.

Following the advice of other route writers and cyclists I have made a few changes to the format of this book from the first two publications. Hopefully this will make the routes easier to follow and the guide simpler to use. Let me know your views. From July 1997 City Slicker Publications is on the Internet with both E-mail and a site on the World Wide Web (see page 2). We can use these to keep each other up to date with news and views on recreational and utility cycling in the north east.

The first good news is that in researching this book I have found enough routes for another guide. This one will feature rides around south and west Durham. Many of the rides will connect with routes in this book and my first two guides. It will be published in early summer 1998.

Acknowledgements

In researching and producing this guide I have been assisted by staff from Durham County and Sunderland City Councils, the Great North Forest, the Tyne & Wear Development Corporation and Sustrans. This book could not have been produced without their guidance and advice. I am also grateful to several individual landowners for their permission to use tracks in this guide. Bikes, equipment and clothing were supplied by Peter Darke Cycles (sponsored by Met helmets), Denton Cycles, Barrie Hopkirks Cycle Centre and the Newcastle Map Centre.

In particular I would like to thank Gary Callum, David Charlton, Peter, James, Chloe and Robert Darke, Colin Davison, Bryn Dowson, John, Carol and Andrew Earl, Simon Graham, David Gray, Kay Halliman, Sue, Dave, Alice and Jenny Hawley, Les Heal, Joanne and Patrick Henry, Colin Hitch, Norman Hopkins, Tony Hopkins, Andrew Hooper, Jill Hopkirk, Alan Jessup, Ted Liddle, Carlton Reid and Phil Storey. Finally, this book would not have been possible without the continued support of Karen, Peter and Zoe, thanks again.

City Slicker Guides

City Slicker Tyneside	ISBN 0 9525593 0 7
City Slicker Goes Upstream	ISBN 0 9525593 1 5
City Slicker Wearside	ISBN 0 9525593 2 3
*City Slicker Durham	ISBN 0 9525593 3 1

*published 1998

City Slicking
In my first book I included extensive sections on bikes, clothing, maintenance, etc. I don't intend to repeat this information but, in response to questions I have been asked, I feel a few notes of explanation will be useful to users of this guide.

Using This Guide
Using other walking and cycling guides I have had the unfortunate experience of becoming hopelessly lost halfway round a route. I don't really mind that much but younger members of the party are sometimes easily discouraged, especially if the weather is poor. For this reason my route descriptions are deliberately very detailed. I realise that this means frequent stops to consult the guide but once you have ridden the route a couple of times you will probably not need to take the guide with you at all. To make things easier the numbered paragraphs in the text correspond to numbered points on the map. The maps are reproduced beside the relevant route descriptions so you can slip the open book into an A4 plastic map cover and only take it out once or twice on a ride to turn over the page.

Route Grading
All of the routes are graded easy, medium or hard. This is not an exact science and I did not want to get bogged down in a complicated classification system. Easy routes are mainly flat with good quality surfacing throughout. They are suitable for all abilities and types of bike and make ideal family rides. Medium routes contain some steeper climbs or rougher surfaces and are generally longer. They are suitable for cyclists with a little experience and longer family outings but not for very young children. Most of the routes in this guide are at this level. Hard routes will have some very steep climbs and contain technically difficult sections such as stream crossings or steep descents. These routes are for experienced cyclists and are best attempted on a mountain or cross/hybrid bike.

Responsibility
As outdoor activities increase in popularity more and more people will use the facilities available. Most off road cycle routes can be used by walkers and many by horse riders. There is plenty of room for everyone but a little mutual understanding and a lot of common sense is required. To many walkers a group of cyclists travelling at 20 m.p.h. towards them can be quite frightening. Horses can be unpredictable when buzzed by speeding cyclists and they not equipped with brakes. Always slow down when passing walkers or riders and give way when necessary. On narrow tracks ride in single file and in very busy areas consider dismounting and walking rather than weaving your way round pedestrians. Remember you represent all cyclists when you are out, take your responsibility seriously.

Respect
All the routes in this book have been carefully researched and are completely legal for cyclists. In researching this guide I have used just about all of the available off road tracks in Wearside. There are lots of other paths and tracks around which can be and are ridden. Some of these are on private land, others are footpaths. Now I realise that many of our laws on land ownership and rights of way are totally out of date and that some other countries adopt a much more liberal attitude to access. However unregulated riding can and will harm sensitive environments. Repeated use on tracks not suitable for cycling will eventually cause erosion and destroy the very thing we are looking for. We all think that we are the only one going this way, but if you've found it then others will. If you want to change things then join a group campaigning to improve access, they will be glad of your support. Collective action is always more effective than individual trespass. In the meantime look after your planet, stay legal and respect the rights of everyone else who has an interest in using, living in, farming, maintaining and enjoying the land.

Types of Rights of Way
A very good booklet on your rights and responsibilities called "Out In The Country" is available from: Countryside Commission Postal Sales, PO Box 124, Walgrave, Northampton, NN6 9TL, Telephone 01604 781848. The following information, taken from this publication, is intended only for guidance and information. The only up-to-date and legal source on rights of way in your area is the definitive map and accompanying statement. These have to be prepared and updated by the county or metropolitan council responsible for the area concerned. You have a right to see both the map and the statement in order to check the status of rights of way.

Footpaths
A footpath may be used only for walking. Strictly speaking you must carry your bike, but I'm sure you can push without any problems. A few of the routes in this guide cross footpaths, mainly on bridges and in underpasses.

Bridleways
These may be used for walking, riding and cycling. Cyclists must give way to walkers and riders. Driving a vehicle is not permitted, even if it is horse-drawn.

Byways
This is a highway that is used mainly for walking, riding horses or cycling. There is also a right to use any kind of wheeled vehicle on byways.

Green Lanes
This term has no legal meaning.

Roads Used As Public Paths (RUPPs)
The exact status of these is very ambiguous and they are currently all being reclassified. However you have at least the same rights on a RUPP as on a bridleway.

Public Roads
It is usually safe to assume that that you can drive, walk or ride along those roads and lanes that are shown in colour on Ordnance Survey maps, unless there are clear notices to the contrary. Some minor lanes are shown uncoloured and for this reason they are sometimes known as 'white roads'. It will usually be obvious, either from the map or on the ground, whether a particular lane or track is public or private; for instance if it leads solely to a country house or a farm it will be private. Ask your local council for advice if you are not sure.

Permissive paths
A landowner may be willing to let you use other paths and tracks over his land that are not public rights of way. These are termed 'permissive paths' which you do not have a statutory right to use. Often there will be a notice at either end of the route explaining this and outlining any conditions that the owner has set.

Maps
All the routes in this guide are covered by the Ordnance Survey Landranger sheets 88 & 93, but apart from general route planning they do not show enough detail. The OS Pathfinder maps are much better for cyclists. For all Ordnance Survey and a wide range of local and other maps as well as a good selection of guide books the Authorised Dealer is:
The Newcastle Map Centre, 55 Grey Street, Newcastle upon Tyne, Tel: 0191 261 5622
The Map Centre staff have been extremely helpful in my research for this guide. The shop provides an excellent service for all travellers, planners and tourists. I recommend a visit.
To make the routes easier to follow I have included sketch maps. They show the main features of the rides and should be used in conjunction with the route descriptions.

8

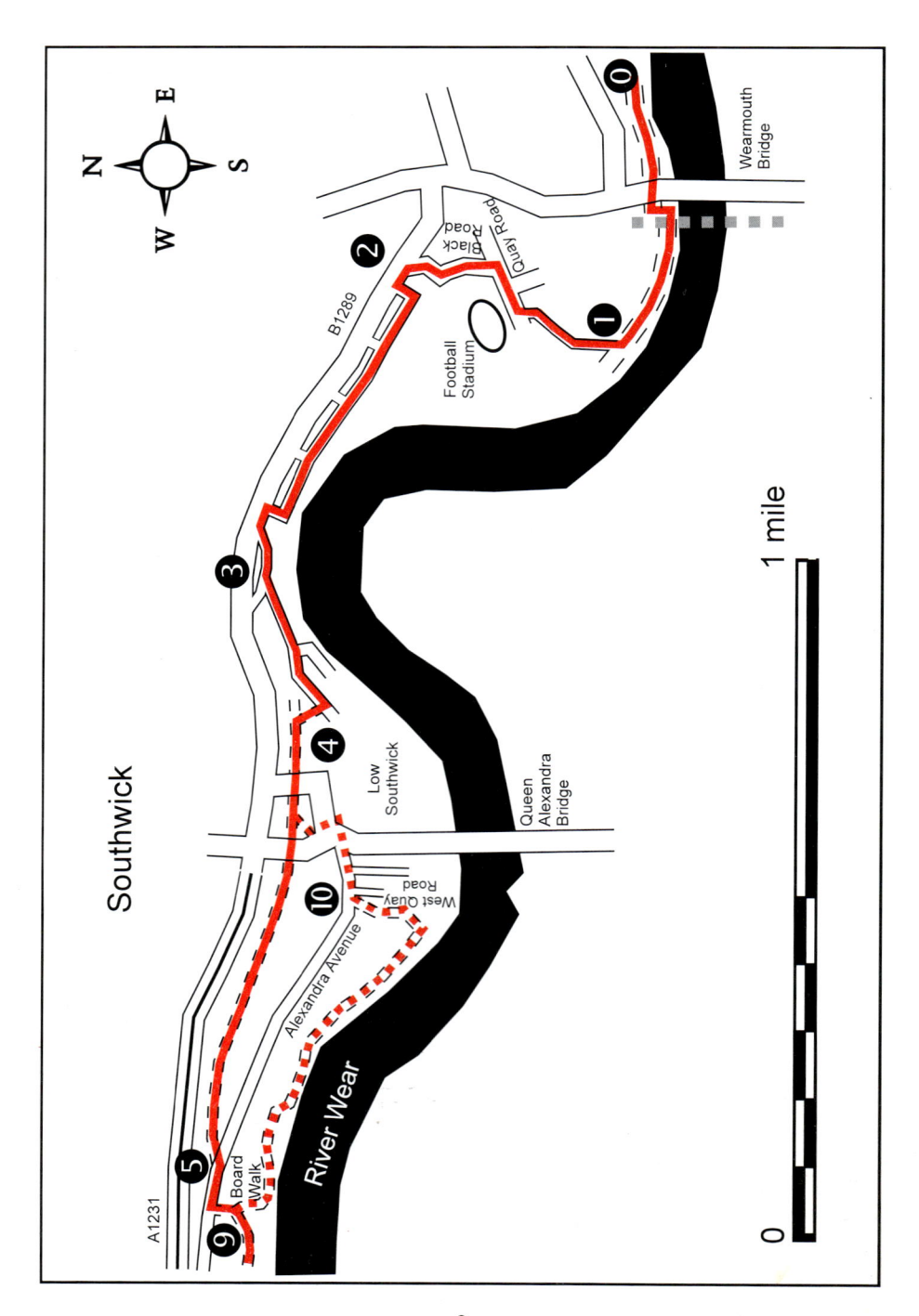

1. Meg the Cockroach
Riverside Trail from Sunderland City Centre to North Hylton via Sunderland Enterprise Park.

Distance:	4.3 miles (6.9 Km.)
Level:	Medium
Maps:	Ordnance Survey Pathfinder 550 Sunderland & 562 Washington & Chester-le-Street
Facilities:	Shops and pubs in city centre and on route. Pub at halfway point
Parking:	Car parks close to the start

Introduction
All I can say is well-done Tyne & Wear Development Corporation. When they took over in 1988 the land here was derelict and scarred from over 200 years of industrial activity. Nearly 10 years and £117 million later the area has changed beyond recognition. In addition to the usual business and industrial developments, the Development Corporation, working with Durham Wildlife Trust, has also made a nature reserve between Baron's Quay and Timber Beach. Artists have created sculptures along the tracks and local schools have contributed poems to be carved into stone and displayed on a poetry walkway.

Hopefully the final leg of the long distance C2C cycle route will soon finish along here so you should meet lots of weary but happy cyclists completing the 140 mile ride from Cumbria.

Route Description

❶ The route starts on St Peter's Riverside. (see Route 2 page 13) Go under the bridges with the River Wear (L) and **TL** onto a red tarmac path. After a short distance fork **L** again and follow the river's edge (L).

(When the Stadium Park area is completed in 1998 a riverside promenade will continue straight on from here giving a ride round one of the most spectacular bends in the river. It will rejoin this route close to the Queen Alexandra Bridge.)

❶ At the cross roads of paths **TR** uphill on a very narrow cobbled lane. This brings you out at the new football stadium where you **TR** onto 'Quay Road' past the stadium (L). At Joan's Cafe **TL** onto 'Black Road'. Cross the bridge to a roundabout at the B1289 with the 'Colliery Tavern' opposite. (This whole area will be changing between 1997 and 1998 with a new road being built along here. However by then the new riverside promenade will be completed making this part of the ride unnecessary.)

❷ **TL** along the footway for 100m then **TL** and **TR** up a back lane. At the end **TR** and **TL** again and pass the 'Halfway House' public house (L). Continue straight on and along a tarmac path for about 100 metres.

❸ **TL** down a path that passes allotments and pigeon crees (L). At the end cross a short muddy track to industrial estate road. About 100 metres further on **TR** up a steep stony ramp that joins a disused mineral line.

❹ **TL** and go through two underpasses to emerge alongside a red sandstone wall (R) with a panoramic view of the riverside and the Queen Alexandra Bridge (L). Continue along the old mineral line until you join 'Hylton Park Road'.

❺ Cross the road at the safe crossing point and a little further on **TL** onto a downhill gravel track past the egg sculpture (R). At the fork (where the alternative route goes SO) **TR** and follow this undulating track until it rejoins 'Hylton Park Road' at a mini roundabout.

10

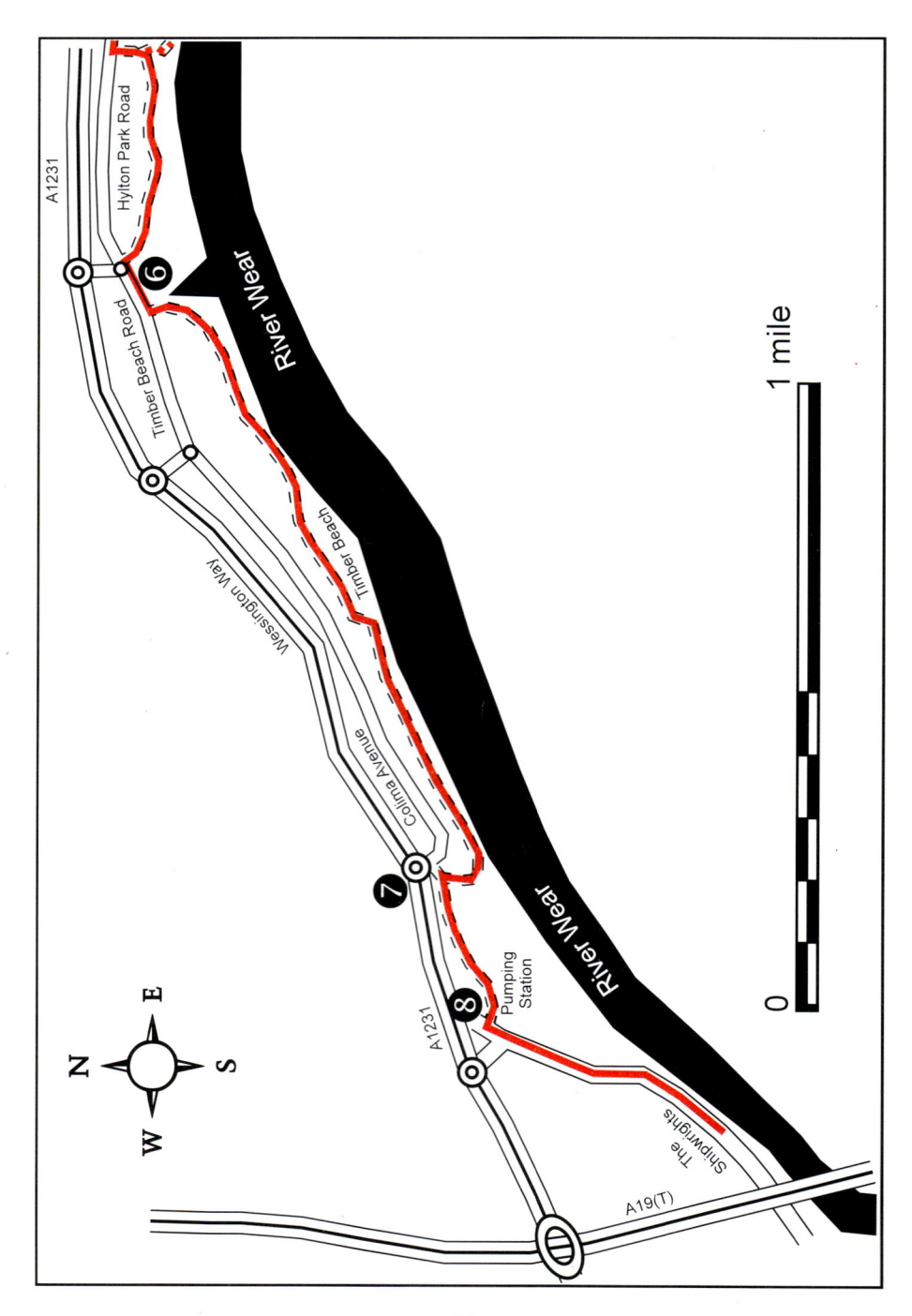

❻ **TL** and follow the footway alongside 'Timber Beach Road'. Just before the first building **TL** through wooden bollards onto a downhill gravel track. Bear **R** at the bottom and follow this track along the riverside, finally bearing **R** uphill away from the river.

❼ At the top **TL** onto a wide gravel track that follows the edge of the A1231(R) for a short while before bearing **L** to pass a pumping station (L).

❽ At the T junction with road **TL** and then **TL** again at 'Tarril Boarding Kennels' onto 'Ferryboat Lane'. This road takes you downhill to the riverside again and the 'The Shipwrights' public house (R). You can turn round here or cycle on a little further until you are under the A19(T). The return journey includes an alternative section along the riverside that is described below.

Alternative Route

❾ At the seat shaped like a shipyard crane, fork **R** steeply downhill. At the bottom bear **L** across wooden walkway and onto a gravel track along the river's edge (R). There is a good view down stream from this path. At the CCTV camera bear **L** and go uphill to the junction of 'Alexandra Avenue' and 'West Quay Road'.

❿ **TR**, cross 'West Quay Road' and continue over second road to the traffic lights. Use the 3 Pelican crossings to cross to the central island and join the gravel track that leads to a T junction with the disused mineral line. **TR** through underpass rejoining the outward route.

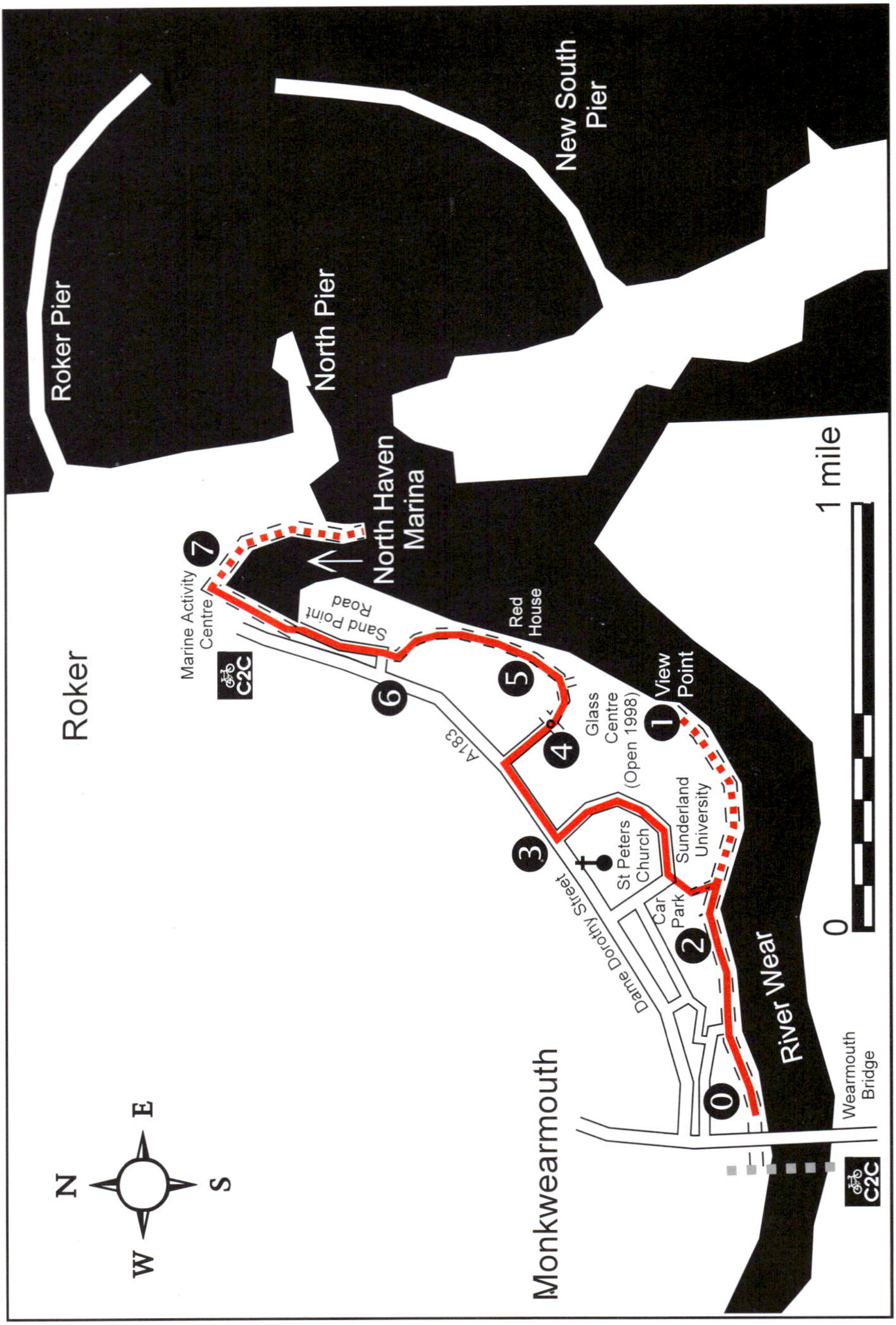
Roker Pier
North Pier
New South Pier
Roker
North Haven Marina
Marine Activity Centre
C2C
Sand Point Road
Red House
A183
Glass Centre (Open 1998)
View Point
St Peters Church
Sunderland University
Car Park
Dame Dorothy Street
River Wear
Wearmouth Bridge
Monkwearmouth
0
1
2
3
4
5
6
7
0
1 mile
N
E
S
W

2. Shattered

Riverside Trail from St Peter's to North Haven & the Marine Activities Centre

Distance: 1.8 miles (2.9 Km.)

Level: Easy

Maps: Ordnance Survey Pathfinder 550 Sunderland

Facilities: Shops and pubs in city centre, on route and at the finish.

Parking: In the City Centre & close to the start.

Introduction

This is the second area of regeneration by the Tyne & Wear Development Corporation in Sunderland. St Peter's has a rich historical heritage. The Anglo-Saxon church that overlooks the University campus is all that remains of a 7th century monastic complex founded by Benedict Biscop. It was here that the young Bede studied.

It was also Benedict Biscop who brought specialists from France to manufacture glass for the new monastery. This is the first evidence of glass making in Britain and the beginning of Sunderland's long association with the craft. This is to be celebrated with the creation of a new £15 million National Glass Centre on the riverside.

The area also features the work of the Riverside Sculpture Project. As you cycle along look out for their many and varied creations. A useful guide to all their locations is available from local information points.

Route Description

0 The route starts on St Peter's Riverside. (see Route 1. page 9) Cycle down the wide promenade with the River Wear (R). Continue past Sunderland University's waterside campus (L) to a viewpoint.

1 The path is blocked here. Eventually, when the stunning new National Glass Centre is built on this site, the promenade will continue along the edge of the river. For the moment you will have to turn back.

2 Just past the University buildings (R) **TR** uphill on a temporary path to the University car park. Cross the car park diagonally to the top R corner and **TR** onto the road that skirts St Peter's Church (L). Follow this road round **L** to a T junction with 'Dame Dorothy Street'.

3 **TR**, but stay on the footway and, at the next mini roundabout **TR** again past the 'Always Open Gates' (R). Continue down to another roundabout.

4 Just across the roundabout you bear **L** past a red sandstone sculpture onto a track that goes downhill bearing **L** at the bottom. (On your R is the junction where the track past the glass centre will join when it is completed)

5 Pass the 'Red House' sculpture (L) and follow the track round **L** and uphill. There are glorious views of the estuary from here (R).

6 At T junction with 'Sand Point Road' **TR** downhill going straight on at the bottom onto the promenade along the North Haven Marina.

7 The Marine Activity Centre is the finish of this ride and also the C2C that started in Cumbria 140 miles away. You can **TR** along the promenade to the Finger Jetty and the viewpoint at the end. To return follow the outward route back to St Peter's Riverside.

13

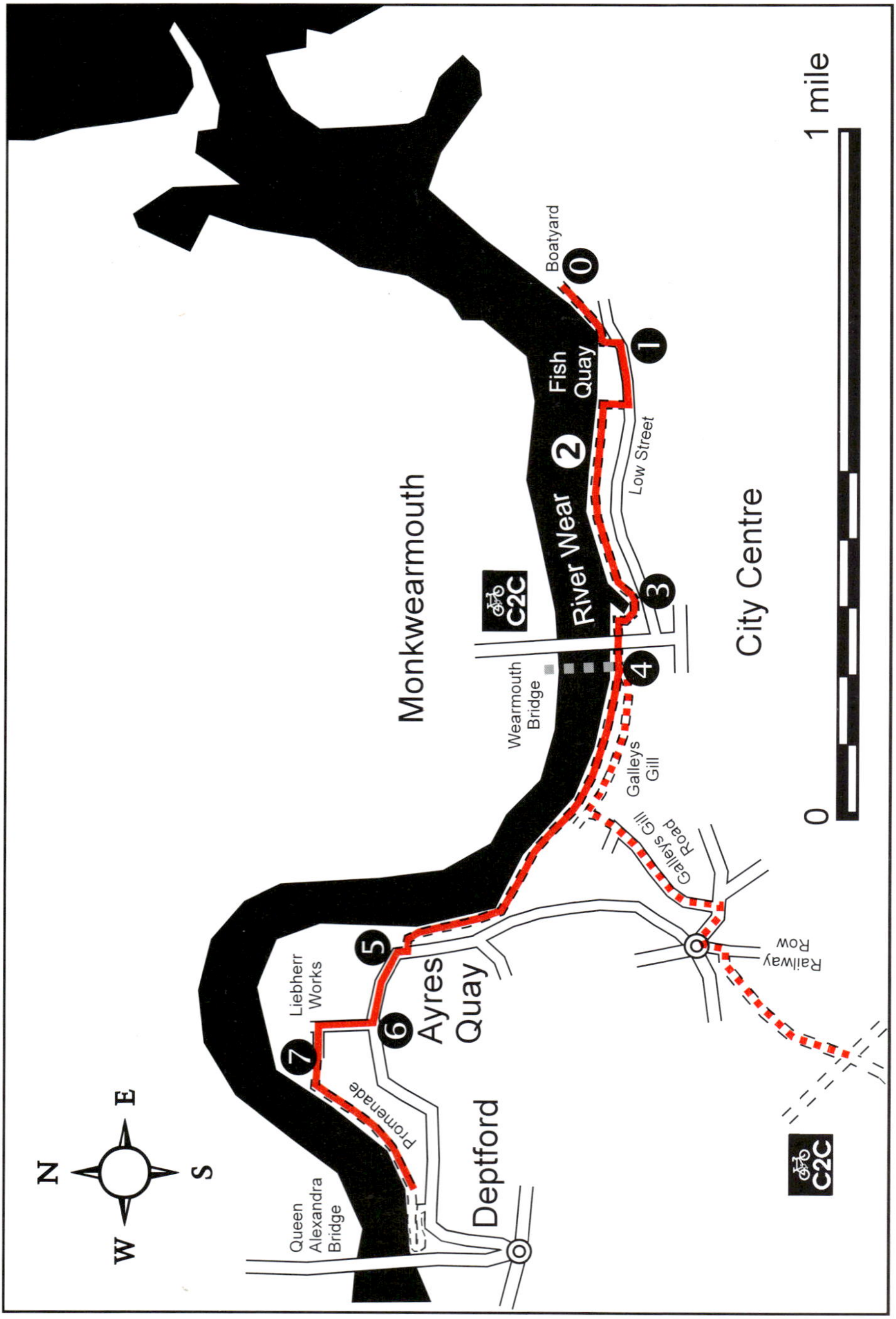

Monkwearmouth
River Wear
Fish Quay
Boatyard
Low Street
City Centre
Wearmouth Bridge
Galleys Gill
Galleys Gill Road
Railway Row
Ayres Quay
Liebherr Works
Promenade
Deptford
Queen Alexandra Bridge
C2C
C2C
0
1
2
3
4
5
6
7
N
E
S
W
0
1 mile

3. Salt, Fish and Microchips

Riverside Trail the Fish Quay to Deptford via Panns Bank & Galley's Gill

Distance: 1.6 miles (2.6 Km.)

Level: Easy

Maps: Ordnance Survey Pathfinder 550 Sunderland

Facilities: Shops and pubs in city centre and on route.

Parking: Car Parks in the city centre & close to the start.

Introduction

The origins of modern Sunderland lie on the south bank of the Wear. Part of the site is a designated Conservation Area and the listed Rosaline and Exchange Buildings are being restored by the Development Corporation.

Sunderland's first major industry, salt refining, started in the Panns Bank area in the late 16th century. By the late 18th century the quayside was home to a small fishing fleet. Coal, timber, lime and grasses used in paper manufacture were all part of the busy riverside trade that flourished after the Industrial Revolution. By the 19th century shipbuilding had become the most significant industry.

In some respects the area has almost come full circle. A monastic seat of learning in the 7th century; the opposite bank is now home to Sunderland University's schools of Business, Computing and Information Systems.

Route Description

0 The route starts by a boatyard as far as you can get along the riverside promenade downstream from the fish quay. Head upstream with the River Wear (R).

1 At the time of writing (April 1997) the Fish Quay is undergoing restoration so you will have to **TL** & **TR** along 'Low Street' past the back of the quay, then **TR** & **TL** back onto the promenade. When the work is finished the promenade will continue along the riverside here.

2 From here your route follows the river's edge, through Brewery Yard, past the beautiful and colourfully restored 'Roseline Building' (L) and the new student halls of residence (L). Look out for the bicycle wheel gates (L).

3 Cycle round the top of the small dock (R) past the bottom of 'Panns Bank' (L). (If you wish to cross to the other side of the river for Routes 1 & 2 (see pages 9 & 13) then you can bear **L** up here to the end of Wearmouth Bridge **TR** and cross the bridge.)

4 Once under the bridges stay on the lower promenade following the river upstream. The area (L) above you is known as Galley's Gill. Finally the path goes uphill towards two tall cranes. Bear **L** at the top to a T junction with road and 'The Winstone' public house (L).

5 **TR** downhill past 'The Saltgrass' public house (L). Pass turnings **L** & **R** before you **TR** through the double metal gates which lead down to the entrance to Liebherr works.

6 **TL** just before works gates onto a road and straight on to a path that takes you back to a riverside promenade.

7 **TL** along the promenade and cycle along to 'The Ropery' public house (L). You can continue past here for a short distance right down to the base of the Queen Alexandra Bridge before turning back for the return journey.

15

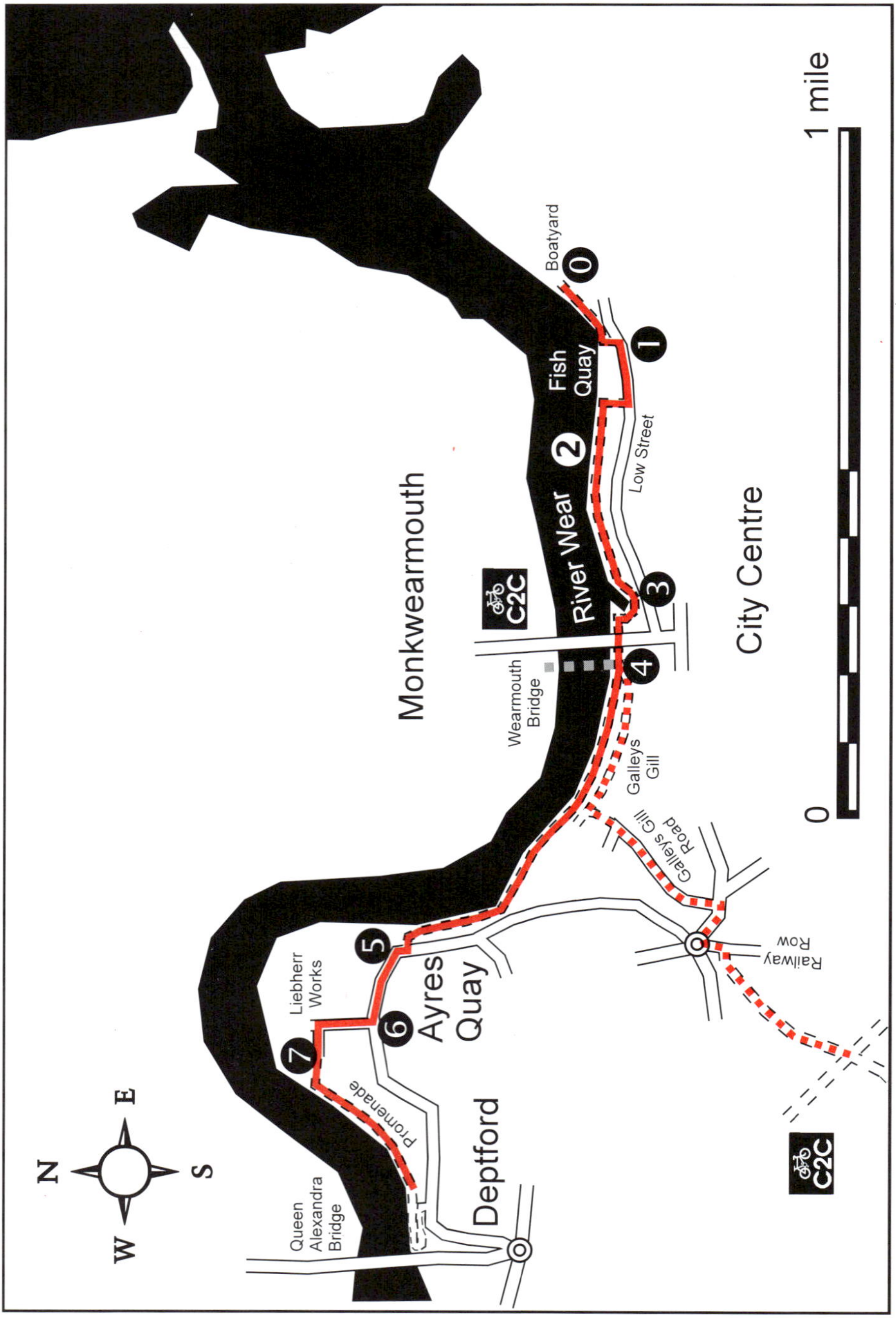

Monkwearmouth
City Centre
River Wear
Fish Quay
Low Street
Boatyard
0
1
2
3
4
5
6
7
Wearmouth Bridge
Galleys Gill
Galleys Gill Road
Railway Row
Ayres Quay
Liebherr Works
Promenade
Deptford
Queen Alexandra Bridge
C2C
C2C
N
E
S
W
0
1 mile

Link Route

This takes you via the old Hetton Colliery Line to the junction with the Penshaw Branch Line. It links with Routes 4 & 5 (see pages 19 & 21) which both take you out of the city centre and to other rides in this guide. It is currently the route of the C2C.

❹ Instead of staying on the low promenade fork **L** and follow the zigzag path uphill and along the top promenade.

❽ At the open area bear **L** on the path under the metal footbridge, through the barrier and uphill on 'Galley's Gill Road' to a T junction with main road A1231. This is a busy road so take care.

❾ **TR**, go up to the roundabout and take the first **TL** off the roundabout into 'Railway Row'. Almost immediately cross this road onto a tarmac path that goes up through a barrier and onto the railway path.

❿ Finish through a barrier to the memorial for the Penshaw and Hetton Railways. Route 4 (see page 19) joins **R** here and Route 5 (see page 21) **L**. Both continue straight on.

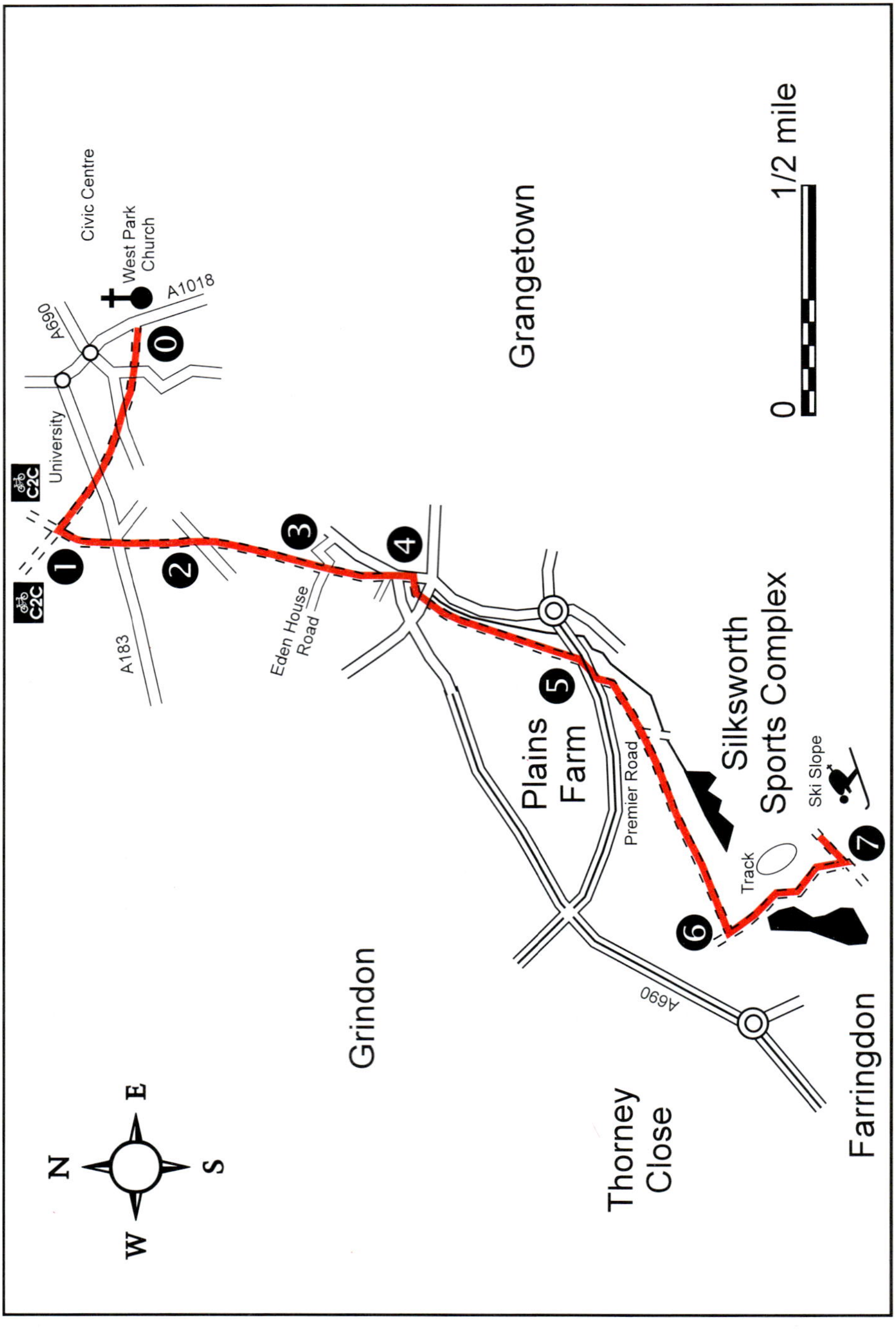
Civic Centre
West Park Church
A1018
A690
University
C2C
A183
Eden House Road
Grangetown
Plains Farm
Premier Road
Silksworth Sports Complex
Ski Slope
Track
Grindon
A690
Thorney Close
Farringdon
N
E
S
W
0
1/2 mile
0
1
2
3
4
5
6
7

4. Station to Station
Sunderland City Centre to Silksworth

Distance:	2.8 miles (4.5 Km.)
Level:	Easy
Maps:	Ordnance Survey Pathfinder 550 Sunderland or 562 Washington & Chester-le-Street
Facilities:	Shops and pubs in city centre and on route. Toilets and changing at Silksworth Sports Centre.
Parking:	Car Parks in the City Centre. Free parking at Silksworth Sports Centre.

Introduction

This ride takes you from central Sunderland to the edge of the city where you can join several other circuits in this book.

It starts along the route of the old Penshaw railway that ran from Penshaw to the South Dock via the Central Station. Opened in 1852, freight and passenger services continued until the line closed in 1964. The second part of the route is on the former Hetton Colliery line (1822 - 1959). This line carried coal from Hetton Lyons over Warden Law and down to staiths on the River Wear.

It's fashionable to be nostalgic about our industrial heritage. On route look out for the cuttings, embankments, bridges and tunnels that remind us of the days when digging coal fed the hungry steam engines, the tired pitmen and the greed of the mine owners.

Route Description

❶ Go through the barriers opposite West Park church and onto the old Penshaw branch line. Follow the wide path until you come to a roundabout with plaques commemorating the Penshaw and the Hetton Colliery Line that passed over here at this point.

❶ **TL** here (TR Route 3, see page 15 or SO/TL Route 5, see page 21) and go down the back lane. At the end bear left down a short path to a road.

❷ Cross road and continue uphill on the path opposite.

❸ Cross 'Eden House Road' and **TL** through gap in the old stone bridge abutment onto the path that continues along an embankment. (TR Route 5) Cross road and continue along the old railway line until the path emerges at a major junction with 'The Barnes' public house opposite.

❹ **TR**, cross 'Richard Avenue' then **TL** and cross the main road using the refuge. Keep 'The Barnes' (R), push past the pub car park on the pavement then immediately **TR** onto a narrow track that goes downhill and under a bridge. The path follows a burn (L) then crosses some open ground finishing uphill to 'Premier Road'.

❺ Cross this dual carriageway carefully and join the wide downhill track opposite. This continues to follow the burn (L) then the edge of the Silksworth Sports Complex (L).

❻ At the T junction of paths **TL** onto the tarmac path and go uphill, past the lake (R) following the main track.

❼ At the top bear **L** to finish in the car park beside the administration centre and the ski slope. (This is the start of Route 6, see page 25) To return turn back and follow the outward route.

19

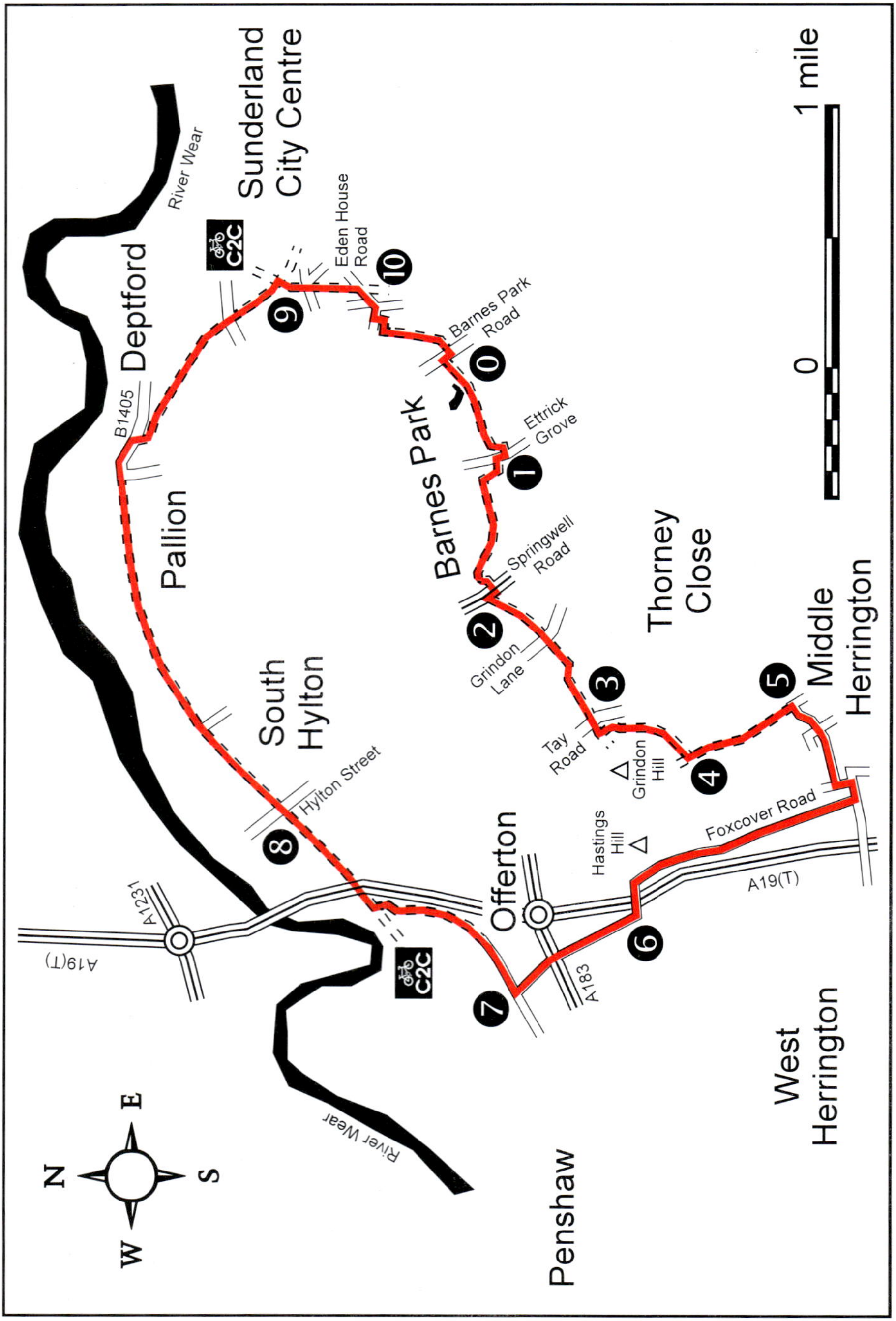
Sunderland City Centre
River Wear
Deptford
C2C
Eden House Road
10
9
Barnes Park Road
0
Barnes Park
Ettrick Grove
1
Springwell Road
2
Grindon Lane
Thorney Close
3
Tay Road
Grindon Hill
4
5
Middle Herrington
Foxcover Road
A19(T)
Hastings Hill
Offerton
6
A183
7
C2C
A19(T)
A1231
8
Hylton Street
South Hylton
Pallion
B1405
River Wear
Penshaw
West Herrington
0
1 mile
N
E
S
W

5. Millenarianism

Sunderland Circuit via Barnes Park, Offerton & Pallion. A *Ride in the 'Great North Forest'*

Distance:	8.9 miles (14.3 Km.)
Level:	Medium
Maps:	Ordnance Survey Pathfinder 562 Washington & Chester-le-Street
Facilities:	Cafes, shops and pubs near start and on route
Parking:	On street parking close to Barnes Park

Introduction

Part of this and the previous route will only be available until the year 2000. It's not that I believe, as some seem to, that the world will end then. However, like the millenarian revolutionaries of the English Civil War, I like the idea of looking forward to a better future on earth. History is linear not cyclic. When we abandon our dependence on the motor car it will be a step into the future not a return to the past. People who advocate this are regarded by many as modern revolutionaries. If that's the case then let's get the revolution started.

The reason is that the section from South Hylton to the city centre will be used for a new extension to the Tyne & Wear Metro system bringing environmentally friendly public transport to the area. All we need to do now is to persuade Nexus to let us take our bikes onto their tramcars. This would reduce our dependence on the car even further.

Route Description

0 As a rule there is no cycling in Barnes Park however Sunderland City Council have kindly granted permission for cyclists to use it when following this route. Please keep to the path indicated and respect the other users of the park. Go up wide road past the pond (R), uphill to a roundabout with trees in the centre. Fork **L**, it is very narrow here so **dismount and push** uphill on the path and out through the park gate. You can go up the steps (R) or continue on and double back to cross the road.

1 Go through the gate into the park opposite. Follow the path **R** downhill and cross 'Barnes Burn'. **TL** and follow the burn (L) up the valley. At the top the path bears **L**, crosses the burn and goes uphill to 'Springwell Road' a dual carriageway. Cross this road with care and **TR**.

2 Just before the school **TL** through gate in a wooden fence onto a tarmac path that crosses open ground ahead. At the next road 'Grindon Lane' **TR** then **TL** through gate. Cross stream and continue to fork in path. Bear **R** here, cross stream again and go on to 'Tay Road'. Cross road to path opposite signposted 'Middle Herrington ¾'.

3 **TL** at crossroads of paths and follow the path round past rear of brick building (L), cross burn and go over cross roads of paths. Follow path past Grindon Hill (R) and houses (L) up to a T junction with field ahead.

4 **TL**, through barrier onto a path that follows the field edge (R). Go through barriers onto a narrow track. Eventually you join a tarmac path that leads into an estate.

5 **TR** onto 'Summerhill', cross 'Steep Hill' and continue downhill to T junction with 'Hillview'. **TL**, go down to T junction and **TR**. Take the next TR, just as you leave the houses, into 'Foxcover Road'. Follow this road up, down and then up again to pass Hastings Hill (R)

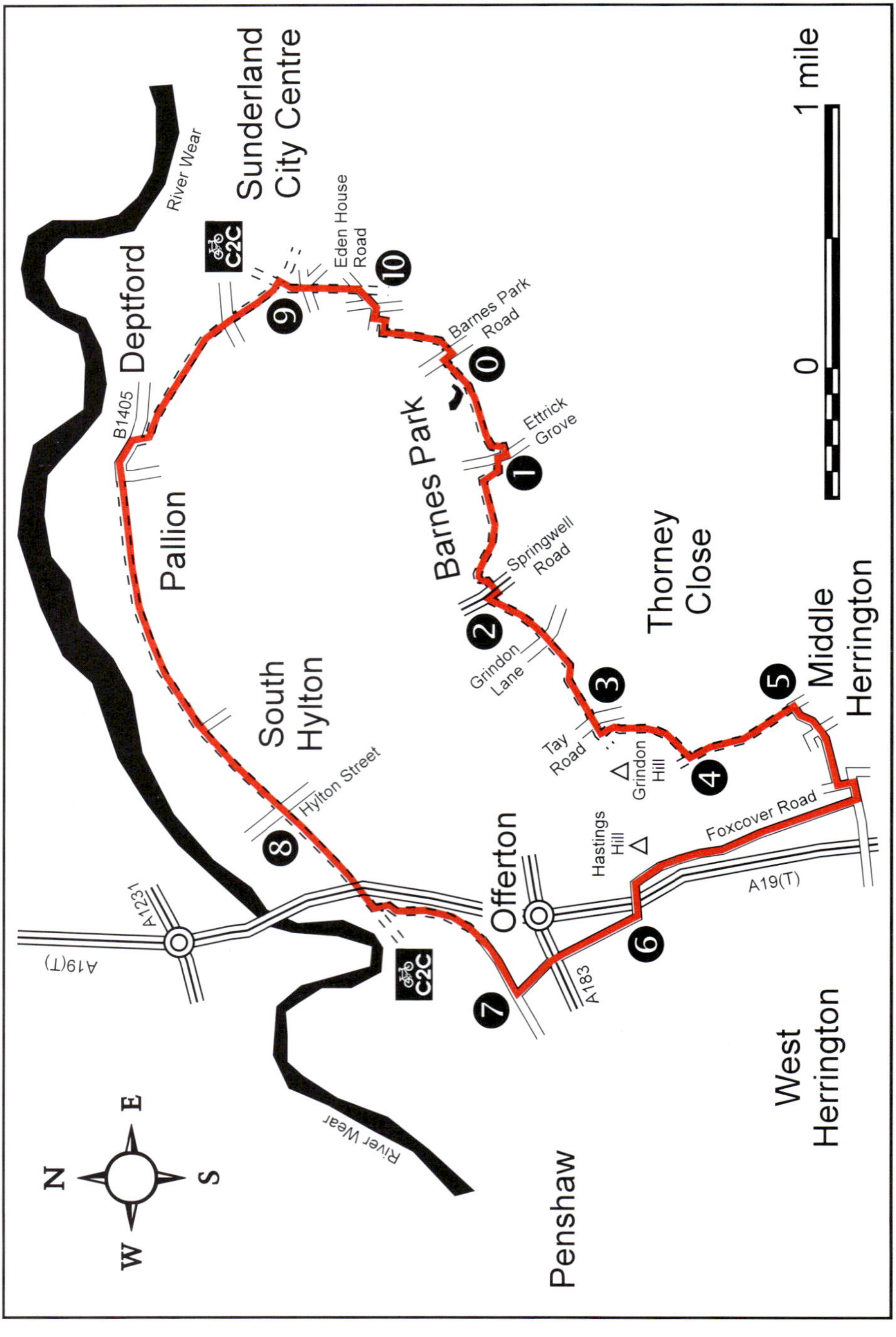
Sunderland City Centre
River Wear
C2C
Eden House Road
10
Deptford
9
Barnes Park Road
0
B1405
Ettrick Grove
1
Barnes Park
Pallion
Springwell Road
Thorney Close
2
Grindon Lane
3
South Hylton
5
Middle Herrington
Tay Road
Grindon Hill
4
Hylton Street
Foxcover Road
8
Hastings Hill
Offerton
A19(T)
A1231
6
A183
7
C2C
A19(T)
West Herrington
River Wear
N
E
S
W
Penshaw
0
1 mile

6 Continue **L** over the A19(T). After the bridge **TR** following the road to a T junction with the A183. Cross the dual carriageway with care and continue down lane opposite to T junction at bottom. (TL/SO Route 8, see page 35) There is a magnificent view of Tyneside and Wearside from here.

7 **TR** and go through Offerton to a gate. Go through this onto 'Offerton Lane' a gravelly path that takes you downhill alongside the A19(T) (R). Take care at the bottom as there is a concrete block just round the last corner. At the T junction (TL Route 8) **TR**, go under the A19(T) and onto the railway path carrying the C2C route towards South Hylton.

8 Cross the next road with 'Hycroft' public house (L) and another road into a cutting. The track goes through a barrier and joins a road (R). Follow this past the Rolls Royce works (R) until the retail park (L) where you cross the road and take the path signposted 'C2C Sunderland City Centre' Follow this tarmac path across the B1405 on old railway bridge to a main road that you cross using the refuge. Continue downhill past 'The Stone Bridge' public house (L), go under a bridge and a little further on you will come to a memorial plaque to the 'Hetton Colliery Railway'. (TL Route 3 see page 15, SO Route 4 see page 19)

9 **TR** here down a back lane and, just before the bottom, **TL** on a path to a main road. Cross the road to the path opposite which goes uphill. At the next main road 'Eden House Road' **TR**. (SO Route 4)

10 Follow this street round to **R** past 'Burnville Road' (R) and 'Hurstwood Road' (L) into 'Hunters Hall Road'. Take the next **TL** past bungalows into 'Nesburn Road'. Just past the last house (R) **TR** and **TL** onto a tarmac path that runs through an open grassy area ahead to a T junction with the B1405. Cross road and **TR** then **TL** into Barnes Park and the finish.

23

24

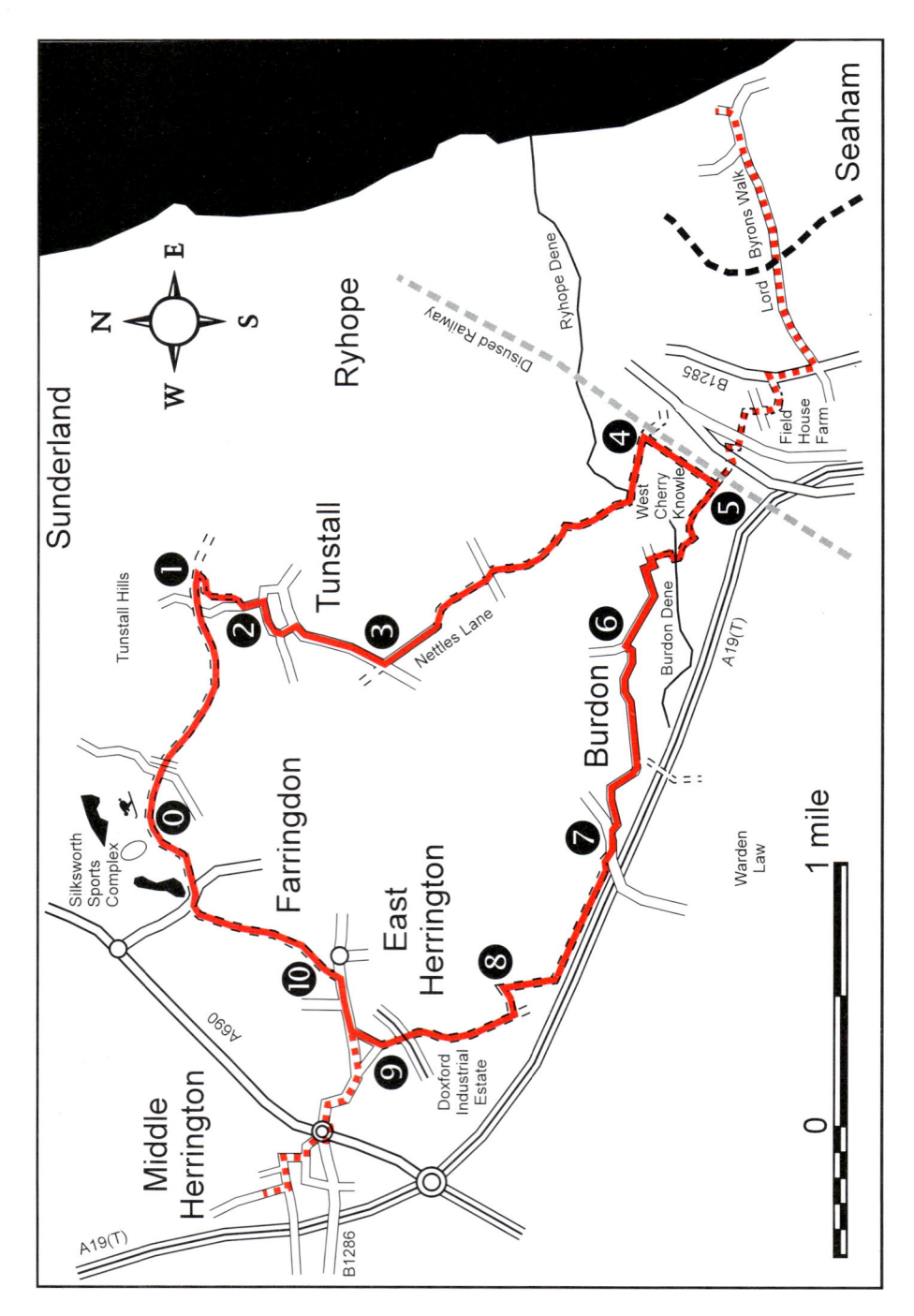

6. Diggers and Levellers

Sunderland Circuit from Silksworth via Tunstall and Burdon
- A Ride in the 'Great North Forest'

Distance:	10.0 miles (16.0 Km.)
Level:	Medium
Maps:	Ordnance Survey Pathfinder 550 Sunderland & Whitburn, 562 Washington & Chester-le-Street
Facilities:	Toilets, showers and changing at the start, shops and pubs on route. Toilets at the picnic site by the coast
Parking:	Silksworth Sports Centre, off the A690 south of Sunderland city centre

Introduction

I can make no claims to have devised this route. It was researched by Ken Maynard and produced by the Great North Forest Project Team. It is reproduced here with their kind permission. I have included a link route to Foxcover Road that connects with two other routes in this guide.

This circuit explores some of the lesser known but attractive countryside to the south of Sunderland. This includes the Tunstall Hills, Cherry Knowle Dene and, if you wish to take the detour, a trip to the seashore near Seaham Hall. Although there are two steep climbs and some of the tracks are a little bumpy it makes a good longer family outing on a warm summer's day. Take a picnic and cool your feet in the North Sea half way round.

Route Description

0 Leave the administration centre (R) keeping the ski slope (R) and **TR** by the children's playground onto a narrow path. Cross the main road at the refuge onto the track opposite which bears **R** downhill onto the disused railway line.

1 After the bridge with two concrete access barriers **TR** onto a cinder track that goes steeply uphill. At the top **TR** through a small gate to join 'Tunstall Hope Road'. **TL** and follow this narrow road uphill to a T junction.

2 TR signposted 'Silksworth' and follow road round to another T junction. **TL** signposted 'Doxford Park B1286' to third T junction and **TR** onto 'Burdon Road'. Pass fire station (L) and continue uphill.

3 Just after the brow of the hill **TL** onto 'Nettles Lane' a single track road that gives you excellent views of the coast. At the cross roads continue straight onto a stony bridleway. Follow this through a series of bends and finally down to cross Cherry Knowle Dene and past West Cherry Knowle farm (R). Go through gate and uphill until you reach the disused mineral line.

4 Do not use the line as the ballast is very uneven in places **TR** just before it and follow the permissive bridlepath up the field edge. This leads you to a T junction with a track. (TL for the link route to the coast)

5 For the main route **TR** and then fork **L** at the electricity pole onto a narrow bumpy track down the field edge. Take care as there is a deep culvert (R) alongside this path. Follow this track round **L** at the bottom of the field, cross ditch **R** on railway sleepers and continue on track round edge of next field. Finally you join a wider track that takes you down to a ford over Burdon Dene. Stay on this track uphill through bends, past Burn Hill Farm (R) bearing **L** onto a tarmac road. Follow this road uphill to fork at Burdon.

25

26

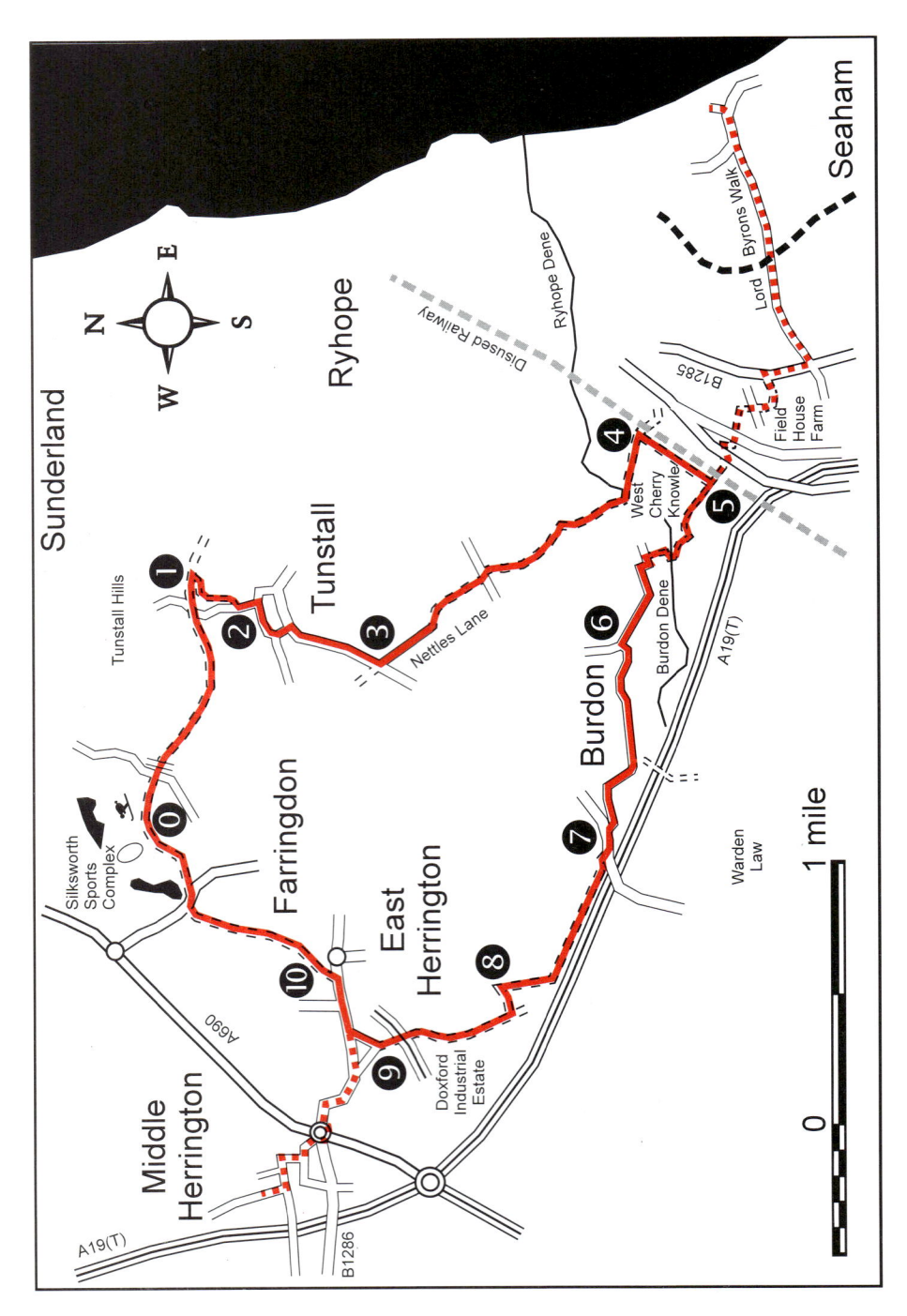

❻ Fork **L** through village and past grounds of Burdon Hall (R). Stay on this road past footpath (L) to Old Burdon Farm that crosses the A19(T) (L) until the T junction at Thristley House Farm.

❼ **TL** then after 100 metres **TR** through barrier onto a gravel track past a sign for the Stephenson Trail. This track follows the A19(T) (L). There are excellent views (R) across Sunderland and Tyneside. Finally you **TR** onto an old mineral line that goes down through trees.

❽ At the bottom follow the main track **L**, past sandstone plaque 'The Ghost of Coal' (R) and up to a T junction with a track. **TR** and follow this narrow track down past the new Doxford Park Industrial Estate. Cross 'City Way' and go down steep bank opposite.

❾ Finally you emerge onto an estate road 'Clinton Place'. **TR** and follow road round to T junction with 'Silksworth Road'. (TL for a link to Route 5 and Route 8, see page 29) **TR** with care and continue past turning to Farringdon (L).

❿ Just past the sign for the roundabout **TL** onto a tarmac path that passes Farringdon School (L). Follow this path, which eventually becomes a stony track past houses (L). Bear R at bottom to main road and cross at the refuge to the main entrance of Silksworth Sports Complex and the finish. The sports complex is also the finish for Route 4 (see page 19).

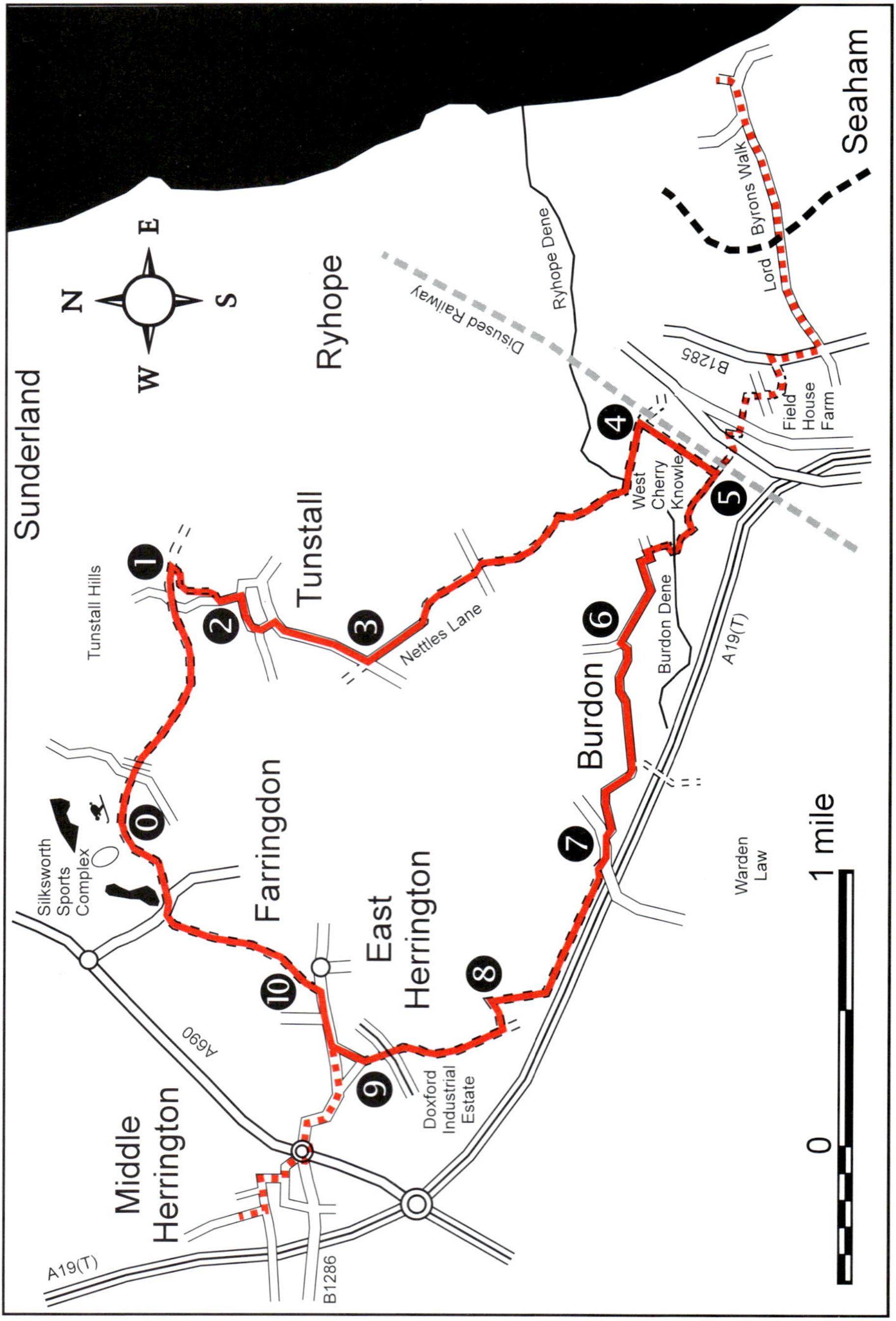
Sunderland
Ryhope
Tunstall
Tunstall Hills
N
E
S
W
Seaham
Ryhope Dene
Disused Railway
Lord Byrons Walk
B1285
Field House Farm
West Cherry Knowle
Burdon Dene
Burdon
A19(T)
Nettles Lane
Farringdon
Silksworth Sports Complex
East Herrington
Warden Law
Doxford Industrial Estate
A690
Middle Herrington
B1286
A19(T)
0
1 mile
0
1
2
3
4
5
6
7
8
9
10

Link Route to the Coast

❺ TL and cross the disused railway line onto a track along the field edge. At the end **TR** and go down through two underpasses.

Cross the new road onto a bridleway that goes down to Field House Farm. **TL** through the farm down a pot holed tarmac road to a T junction with the B1285.

TR up the road to the traffic lights and **TL** onto 'Lord Byrons Walk'.

Follow this road down to the coast and a T Junction. **TR** then **TL** into the car park and picnic area.

To rejoin the main route return the way you came to the disused railway and go straight on.

Link Route to Foxcover Road

❾ At 'Silksworth Road' **TL** and follow the main road to the roundabout with the A690.

Go round the roundabout and **TL** just before the 'Board Inn' public house onto 'Crow Lane' a quiet side street.

TR onto 'Foxcover Lane' and follow this road round **L**. Pass 'Hillview Lane' (**L**) (Route 5, see page 21) and take the next **TR** onto the single track road 'Foxcover Road'. (Route 5, see page 21 and Route 8, see page 35)

29

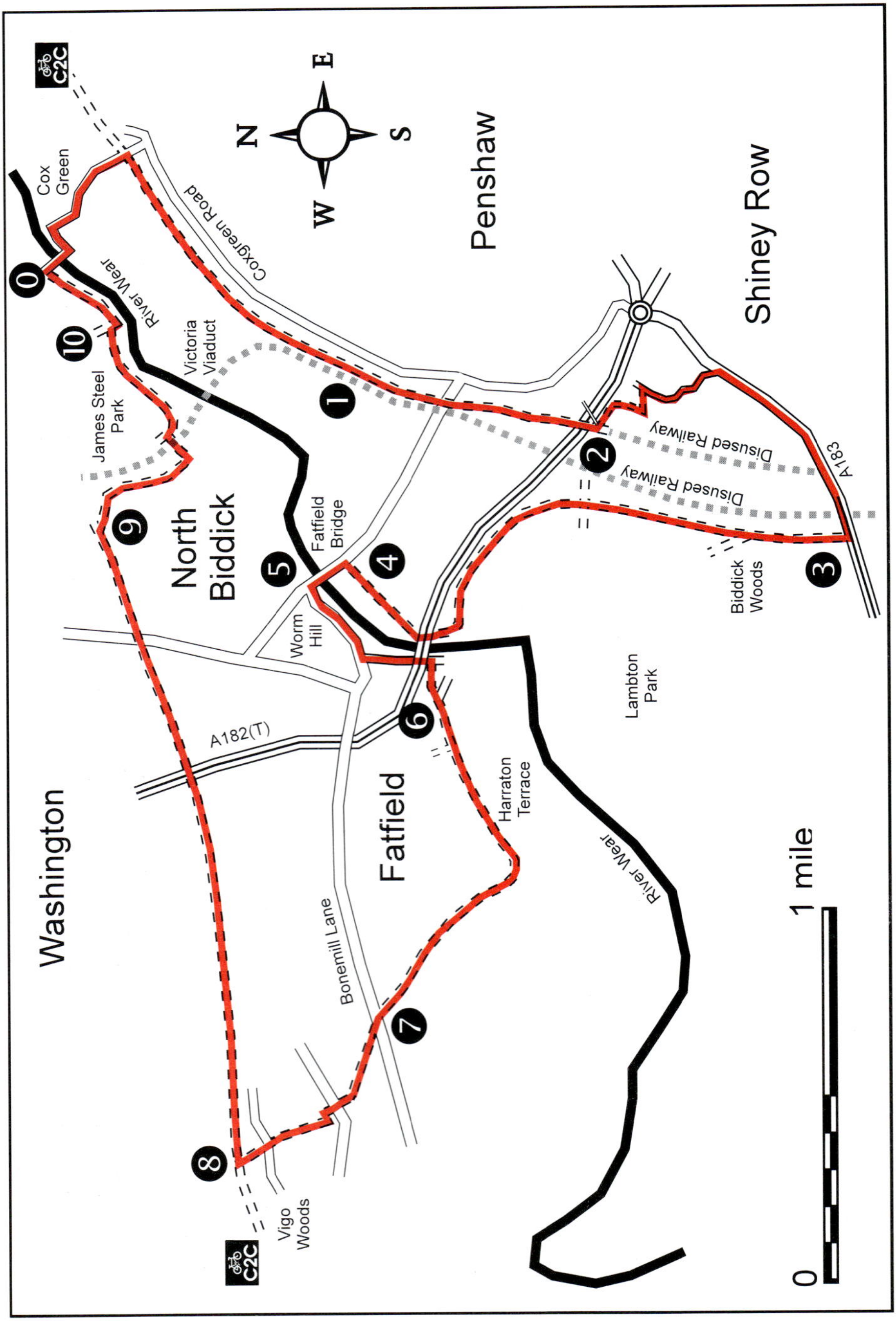
C2C
Cox Green
River Wear
Coxgreen Road
Victoria Viaduct
N
E
S
W
Penshaw
Shiney Row
James Steel Park
North Biddick
Fatfield Bridge
Disused Railway
Disused Railway
A183
Biddick Woods
Worm Hill
Lambton Park
A182(T)
Fatfield
Harraton Terrace
River Wear
Washington
Bonemill Lane
Vigo Woods
C2C
0
1
2
3
4
5
6
7
8
9
10
0
1 mile

7. The Lion and the Worm
Circuit via Shiney Row, Fatfield and North Biddick
A Ride in the 'Great North Forest'

Distance: 10.3 miles (16.5 Km.)

Level: Easy

Maps: Ordnance Survey Pathfinder 562 Washington & Chester-le-Street

Facilities: Pubs and shops on route in Shiney Row, North Biddick and Fatfield.

Parking: James Steel Park, near Swan and Pattison Industrial Estate, Washington

Introduction

The legend of the Lambton Worm tells of a beast that terrorised this area. Its strength was that when cut, the wounds healed themselves. Finally 'brave and bold' John Lambton, after consulting a wise woman for advice, cut it in half while standing on a rock in the middle of the River Wear. The bits floated away and could not join up. Unfortunately, he did not keep a vow he made to kill the next living creature he saw, which turned out to be his father, and brought a curse onto the Lambton family.

This is a really great story for dragon lovers and aristocrat haters. Perhaps the curse still has some power. Lambton Park was the venue for an ultimately unsuccessful and plainly ridiculous venture in the 1960s - a safari park - complete with African animals roaming the chilly parkland.

Route Description

O Leave the car park (see 'City Slicker Goes Upstream' Link Routes 2 & 3) and cross the River Wear on the footbridge. At the end **TL**, then just before the 'Oddfellows Arms' **TR** signposted 'Cox Green Station'. Follow this road uphill to the disused railway line and the C2C route (L). (SO/TL Route 8, see page 35) **TR** onto the line.

1 Soon you will be travelling parallel with another railway line (R). Continue to the caravan park (L) where the path forks. Keep **L** uphill, fork **L** at the top and descend onto a wide disused railway track. Finally the path crosses the A182(T) on a bridge to a T junction.

2 **TL** and just before the footbridge back over the A182(T) fork **R** onto a stony track. At the top go through the gap in the fence and cross the grassy field to the gate at the corner. Through the gate **TR** onto 'Claremont Road' and follow this through the estate to the T junction. **TR** along the A183, youngsters may be able to use the footpath with care. As the road leaves the houses it becomes dual carriage way and soon crosses the railway line that you followed earlier.

3 Just past the bridge **TR** onto a tarmac bridleway. Bear **R** at the fork onto a track that takes you through the lovely Biddick Wood. The area (L) is the edge of the extensive Lambton Park. Cross the estate road and continue on a narrower track. Take care here as this stretch is very popular with horse riders. Soon the track turns parallel with the A182(T) then curves down to join the Wear (L). Go under the A182(T) and continue on tarmac path that leads to a road with a new housing estate (R).

4 At the T junction **TL** and cross the River Wear on Fatfield Bridge. Just ahead (R) is 'Worm Hill' where the mythical beast is supposed to have rested while it digested its meals of cows and lambs and sheep.

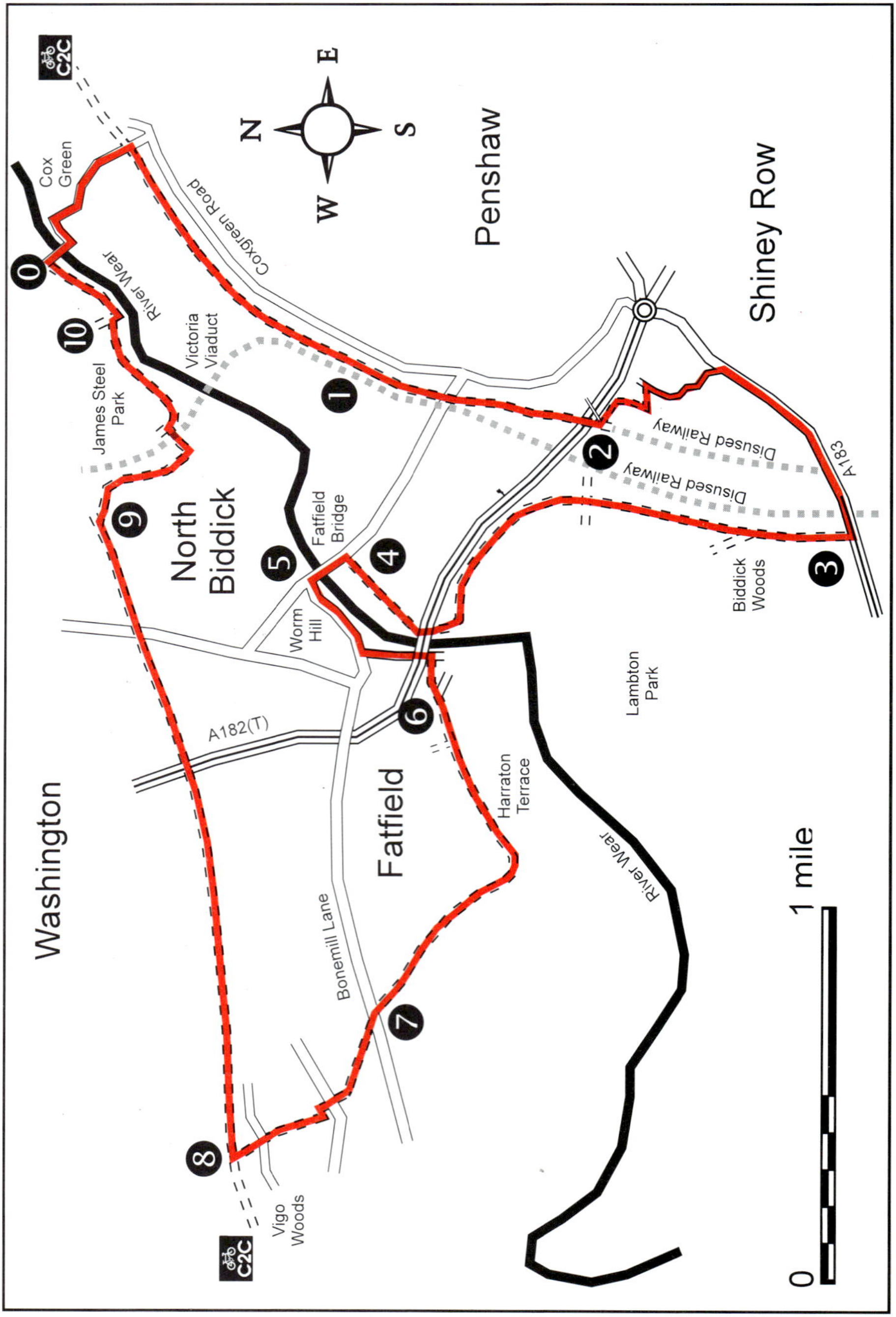
C2C
Cox Green
River Wear
Coxgreen Road
N
E
S
W
Penshaw
Shiney Row
Victoria Viaduct
James Steel Park
North Biddick
Fatfield Bridge
Worm Hill
Disused Railway
Disused Railway
A183
Biddick Woods
Lambton Park
A182(T)
Washington
Fatfield
Harraton Terrace
River Wear
Bonemill Lane
Vigo Woods
C2C
0
1 mile
0
1
2
3
4
5
6
7
8
9
10

❺ Take first **TL** and pass three public houses (R). At the 'North Biddick Club' **TL** into a car park and picnic area. At the end bear **L** onto a tarmac path that follows the river (L). At the end of the flyover under the A182(T) **TR** onto a narrow path between bushes.

❻ This leads to a road marked 'No Entry Except for Access'. Go up this single track road past 'Harraton Terrace' (L), through gate until a junction where the main road enters the Lambton Estate (L). Fork **R** onto a bridleway and continue past playing fields (L) to T junction with 'Bonemill Lane'.

❼ Cross the road bearing **L** onto a tarmac path that crosses field. All of the next section is footpath so you should push your bike. At the top bear **R** then **L** to pass modern church (L) to road. Cross road into a shopping precinct and immediately **TL** then **TR** onto a wide straight path that follows woods (L). At the end cross road onto path through Vigo Wood. After about 100 metres the track climbs the embankment and drops onto the Consett to Sunderland railway line and the C2C.

❽ **TR** onto this good quality track. Soon you will cross the A182(T) for the last time. Pass school fields (L) and cross road continuing on track opposite. A little further on leave the railway bearing **R** through metal bollards then **L** on path by allotment gardens (L).

❾ Follow the railway line (L) then bend down into car parking area. **TL** under bridge to T junction. **TR** downhill with Penshaw Monument ahead. Pass pond (L) and continue on the path through parkland.

❿ At T junction **TR** downhill through barrier past cottages (R). **TL** at the T junction and after 50 metres **TR** towards the River Wear. **TL** and follow the river (R) to the car park at James Steel Park.

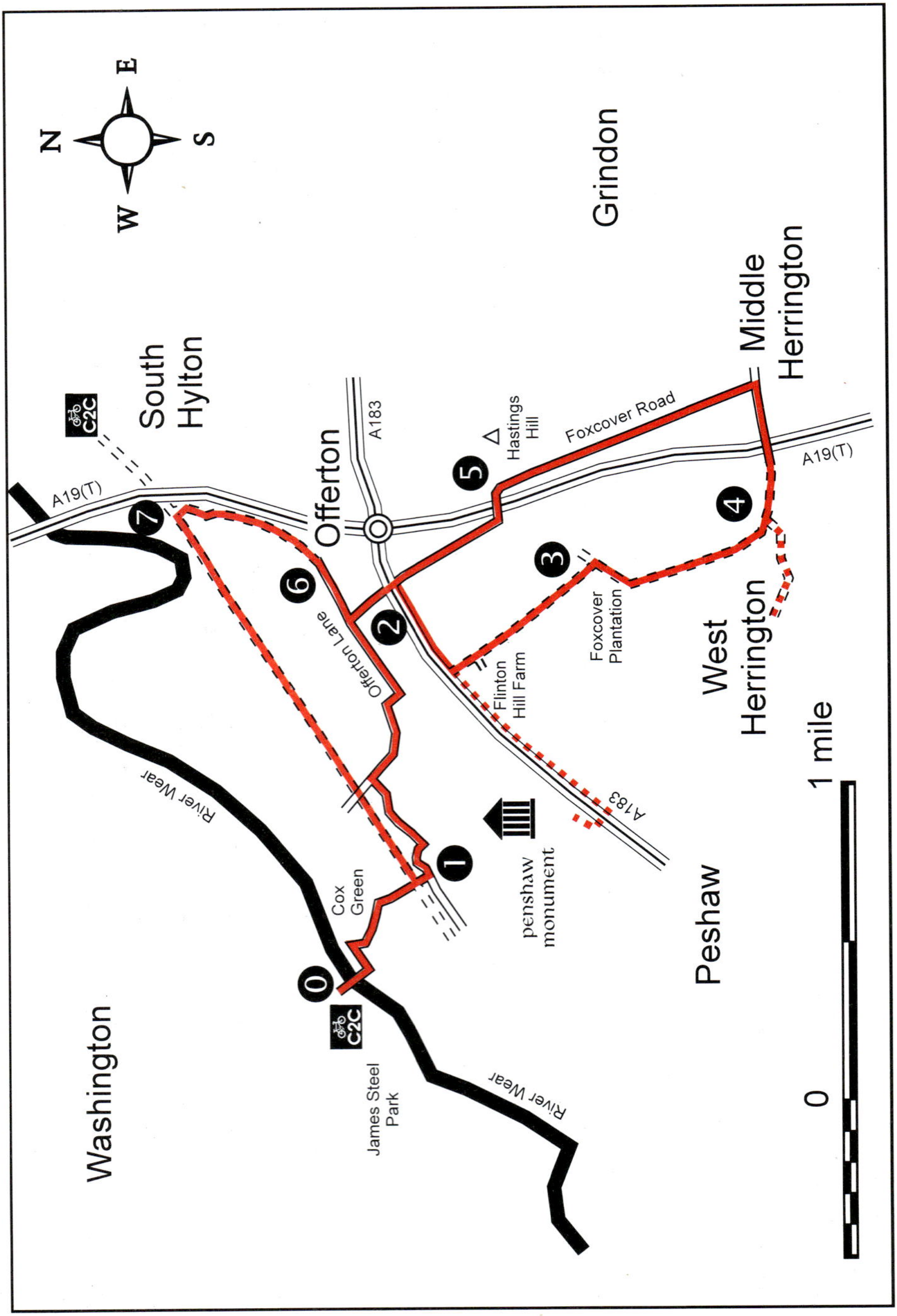

N
E
S
W
Grindon
South
Hylton
C2C
Middle
Herrington
Hastings
Hill
Foxcover Road
A183
A19(T)
Offerton
Offerton Lane
Foxcover
Plantation
Flinton
Hill Farm
West
Herrington
1 mile
0
River Wear
Cox
Green
penshaw
monument
Peshaw
Washington
James Steel
Park
1
2
3
4
5
6
7
0

8. Arthur Was Right
Circuit via Penshaw, Herrington and Offerton
A Ride in the 'Great North Forest'

Distance:	8.1 miles (13.0 Km.)
Level:	Medium
Maps:	Ordnance Survey Pathfinder 562 Washington & Chester-le-Street
Facilities:	Pubs at Cox Green and West Herrington
Parking:	James Steel Park, near Swan and Pattison Industrial Estates, Washington

Introduction

This route will be much better in a few years time when the reclamation works round Herrington Pit are completed. In addition, if the old mineral lines south of Philadelphia are developed, this will open up links to the network of routes round Hetton and Houghton.

I first rode this route with a friend Gary Callum. He worked for British Coal until he was made redundant in 1980s. He served his apprenticeship at New Herrington Pit and, as we rode around he pointed out the terraced home of his grandparents and where he used to play as a child. We followed the road he used to walk up in the early hours of the morning when the new apprentice's job was to knock up the men working on the early shift. Places like New Herrington now seem oddly left behind by the enterprise culture.

Route Description

⓿ Leave the car park (see 'City Slicker Goes Upstream' Link Routes 2 & 3) and cross the River Wear on the footbridge. At the far end **TL** then just before the 'Oddfellows Arms' **TR** signposted 'Cox Green Station'. Follow this road uphill and cross the disused railway line and the C2C (L). (TR Route 7, see page 31)

❶ At the T junction **TL** signposted 'Offerton ½'. At the next junction **TR** signposted 'Offerton 1'. The road climbs steeply and there are excellent views across Tyneside and Wearside (R). At the top of the hill with a farm at the corner **TR** (SO Route 5, see page 21) and go up to the very busy dual carriageway A183.

❷ Cross with care and **TR** onto the path alongside the main road (R). After about 500 metres **TL** onto a public bridleway.

(If you want to take a short detour here you can continue along the A183 for another ½ mile to visit Penshaw Monument. Built in 1844 in memory of the reformer John George Lambton, it is modelled on the Temple of Theseus in Athens.)

At the entrance to 'Flinton Hill Farm' (R) go over a log and onto a straight downhill track. Off R are the extensive remains of Herrington Pit now being landscaped and retored for recreational use. Future cycle routes are planned for this area.

❸ At the T junction **TR** downhill through Foxcover Bank Plantation. Fork **L** and follow track down field edge (R). At the T junction the main route goes **L** although you can **TR** and go uphill into West Herrington for a break at the 'Leg of Mutton' public house (R). There is the possibility of a route from here through West Herrington and either back up to Penshaw or on to Shiney Row, but these will have to wait for reclamation work to be completed.

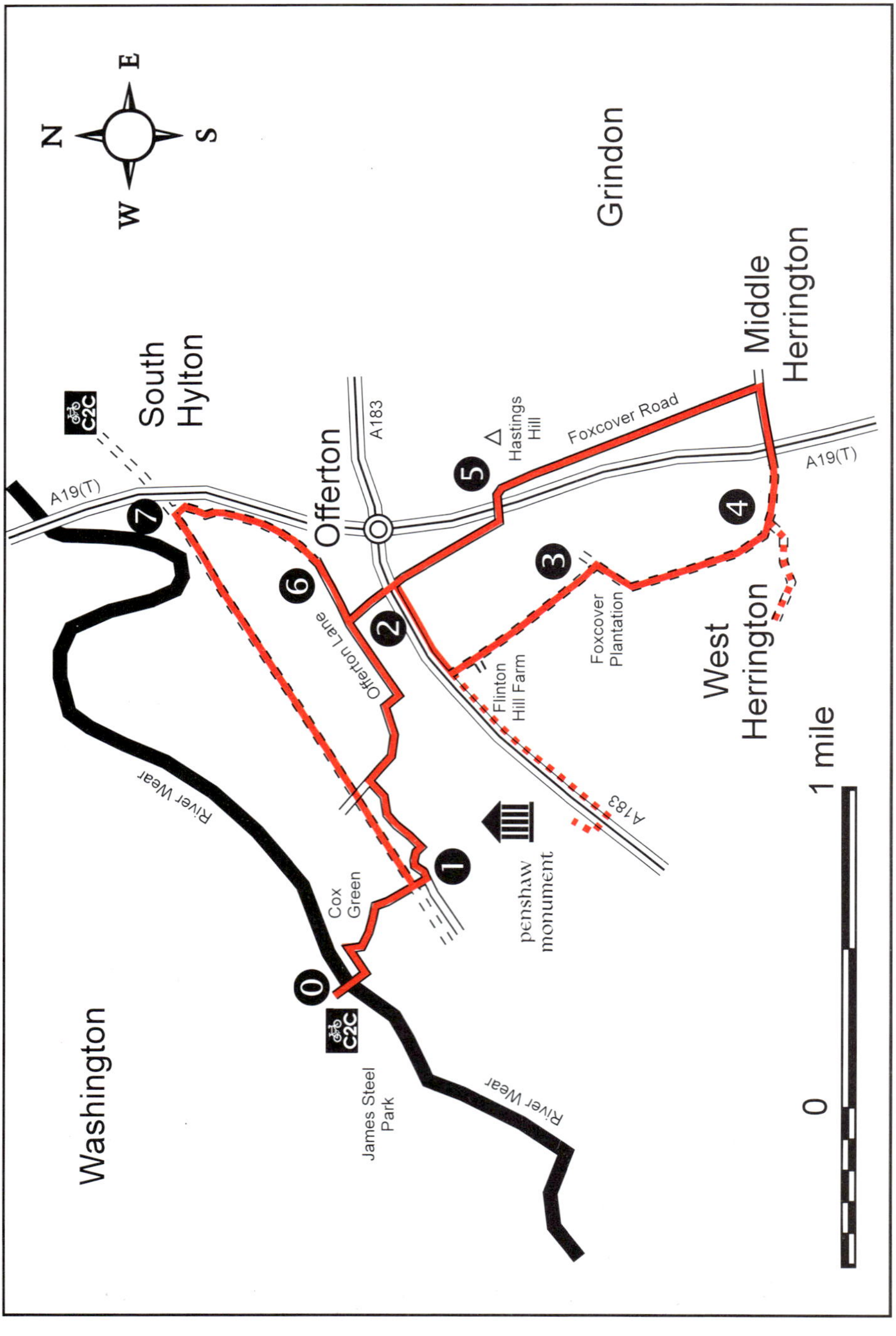
N
E
S
W
Grindon
South
Hylton
C2C
A19(T)
A183
Offerton
Hastings
Hill
Foxcover Road
Middle
Herrington
A19(T)
Offerton Lane
Flinton
Hill Farm
Foxcover
Plantation
West
Herrington
River Wear
Cox
Green
penshaw
monument
A183
Washington
C2C
James Steel
Park
River Wear
0
1 mile
0
1
2
3
4
5
6
7

4 Following the main route **TL** and go up and over the A19(T). Take the next **TL** onto 'Foxcover Road'. (Route 5, see page 21 and a link from Route 6, see page 25 join here) Follow this single track road up, down and then up again to its highest point past Hastings Hill (R).

5 Stay on 'Foxcover Road' and bear **L** to cross the A19(T). At the T juction at the end of the bridge **TR** and follow the lane down to the A183 dual carriageway. Cross with care and go down the lane opposite (this is the way you came up at the start of the ride).

6 **TR** at the T junction onto 'Offerton Lane' into the little hamlet of Offerton. Continue through gate onto a public bridleway signposted 'South Hylton'. Although this narrow twisting downhill track is great fun to ride watch out for horse riders and pedestrians as it is a popular route. Go over the barrier at the end to join the C2C Route. (TR Route 5, see page 21).

7 **TL** onto the disused railway track for nearly 1½ miles until you reach the buildings (L) and the road at Cox Green Station. (SO Route 7, see page 31)

1 You are now back on the outward route. **TR** and follow the road downhill to the 'Oddfellows Arms' (R). **TL** then **TR** to cross the River Wear on the bridge that brings you back to James Steel Park and the finish.

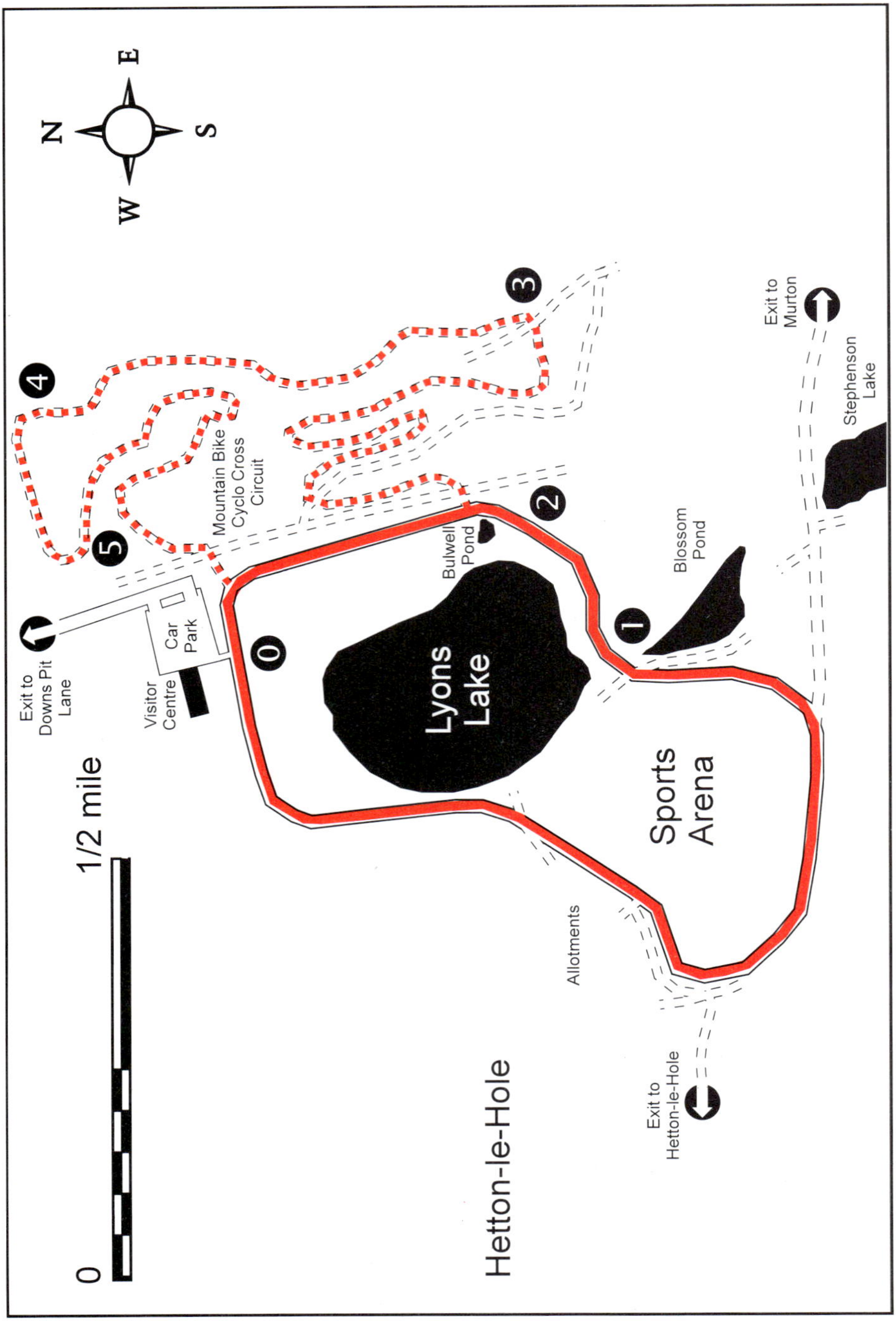

N
E
S
W
1/2 mile
0
Exit to Downs Pit Lane
Visitor Centre
Car Park
Mountain Bike Cyclo Cross Circuit
Bulwell Pond
Lyons Lake
Blossom Pond
Sports Arena
Allotments
Hetton-le-Hole
Exit to Hetton-le-Hole
Exit to Murton
Stephenson Lake
0
1
2
3
4
5

9. You Have Nothing to Lose But Your Chains

Hetton Lyons Circuit 1. Hetton Lyons Park
A Gateway to the 'Great North Forest'

Distance:	1¼ - 3 miles (2.0 - 4.8 Km.)
Level:	Easy (Mountain Bike Circuit: Hard)
Maps:	Ordnance Survey Pathfinder 572 Durham
Facilities:	Toilets, changing facilities, hot & cold drinks in the park's Visitor Centre, 10.00am - 4.00pm (not bank holidays)
Parking:	Car Park in the Country Park

Introduction

Hetton Lyons Country Park offers a wide range of opportunities for recreational use including: angling, cycling, orienteering, equestrian activities and water sports. The park is run by Sunderland City Council. It covers 100 acres of reclaimed land, part of which was the former Hetton Colliery.

The sinking of Hetton Colliery in 1820 through a thick layer of Magnesian limestone was considered a pioneering venture at the time. Many experts thought that no coal deposits existed underneath limestone. After two years of digging the main coal seam was reached at a depth of 654 feet, followed five months later by another seam 234 feet lower. This success paved the way for other mining operations where limestone had previously been considered a serious problem.

Now the park is pioneering activity of a different sort. If you enjoy cycling here then try the three other routes in the guide that start from the Lyons Park. (see pages 41, 43 & 47)

Facilities in the Park for Cyclists

The specialist cycling facilities within the park provide opportunities, both for the novice and experienced cyclists. The purpose built closed circuit cycle track is 1.8 Km long and has a special anti-skid surface. There is also a 3 Km. mountain bike and cyclo-cross track. Cycle ride leaflets are available from the Visitor Centre. Mountain bikes are available for pre booking by groups and organisations.

Route Description

0 Leave the car park by the administration building and **TR** onto the tarmac cycle track. You are now riding round the perimeter of the park past Lyons Lake (L). As you climb the hill take care as there are several pedestrian crossing points.

1 Follow the track round to pass Blossom Pond (R). Stay on the track to Bulwell Pond (L).

2 For the easy ride stay on the main cycle track to the car park and the finish. (1¼ miles). To follow the mountain bike circuit **TR** and leave the tarmac track. Follow the grass track steeply up past the mound (L). Bear L along the second ridge, cross the gravel bridle path and zigzag uphill keeping on the mown grass track.

3 At the top of the hill **TL**, follow the route alongside the path (R) climbing to the highest point in the park.

4 From here **TL** downhill towards the access road. Take care as you ride down through a series of bends as the track here is designed for competitions and is bumpy.

5 Follow the track as it cuts through the grass over the mound and very steeply down to the car park. If this is too steep then cycle along the top of the mound, **TR** down to the main track and **TR** to follow this to the finish.

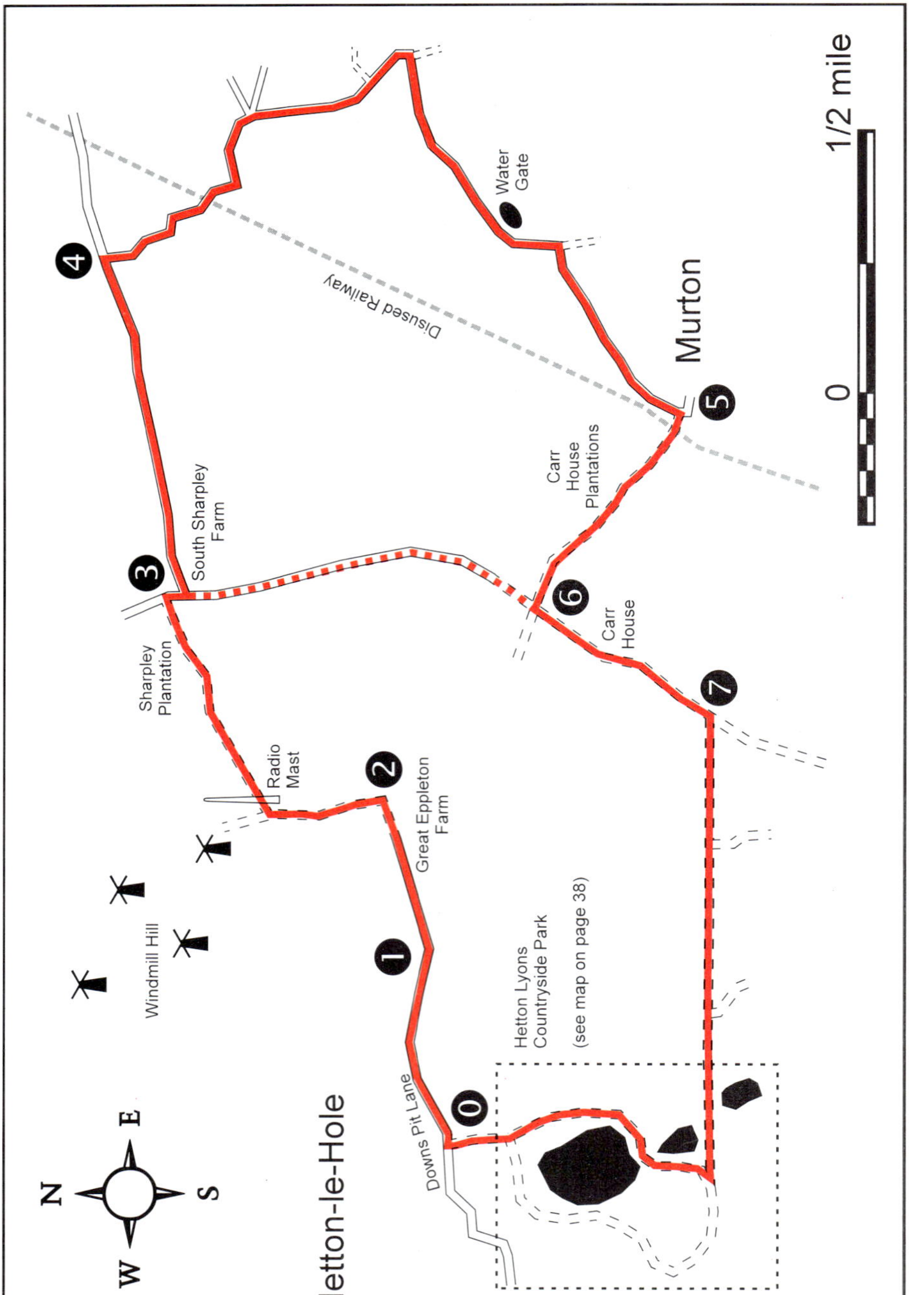
Hetton-le-Hole
N
E
S
W
Windmill Hill
Downs Pit Lane
0
1
2
3
4
5
6
7
Great Eppleton Farm
Radio Mast
Sharpley Plantation
South Sharpley Farm
Disused Railway
Water Gate
Murton
Carr House Plantations
Carr House
Hetton Lyons Countryside Park
(see map on page 38)
0
1/2 mile

10. Wild is the Wind
Hetton Lyons Circuit 2 via Eppleton and Murton
A Ride in the 'Great North Forest'

Distance:	6.4 miles (10.3 Km.)
Level:	Easy
Maps:	Ordnance Survey Pathfinder 572 Durham
Facilities:	Pubs & shops in Hetton. None on route
Parking:	Hetton Lyons Park, off Downs Pit Lane Hetton-le-Hole

Introduction

This ride was originally devised by Sunderland City Council and the Great North Forest team. It was researched by Gary Charlton and John Rostron.

Without Gary the 'City Slicker' series of guides probably would have never got started. Three years ago, with the idea of publishing a cycling guide, I met Gary who not only gave me encouragement but persuaded the Great North Forest to support the project. This encouraged several local councils to give me help and the success of City Slicker Publishing is the result.

This is one of the more challenging routes graded as easy. It is a good one to graduate to after the easy routes around the centre of Sunderland. The only climb is right at the start and Water Gate is an excellent place to stop for a picnic. The route has been recently enhanced by the building of four impressive windmills close to Great Eppleton.

Route Description

❶ Leave the car park heading north to the entrance from 'Downs Pit Lane' and **TR** up steep hill.

❶ Pass the quarry entrance (L) going straight onto a lane signposted 'Public Bridleway East Murton 1¾', past farm at Great Eppleton (R) onto a wide, stony dolomite track.

❷ At the junction **TL** and follow the dolomite track towards the windmills. Just past the tall aerial **TR** onto a grassy track down field edge and under power lines. At the bottom go through gate and along narrow path at the edge of Sharpley Plantation (L). Follow this track up to T junction with narrow road.

❸ **TR** and just before South Sharpley farm **TL** (Go SO here for the short cut). On a clear day there are good views of the coast from this road.

❹ After about ¾ mile **TR** onto single track road that crosses a disused railway line and passes farm buildings. Stay on the road through two sharp bends and past the lake at Water Gate (L). Eventually the road joins the houses at Murton.

❺ **TR** over disused railway. Go through barrier, down field edge, through second barrier and into Carr House Plantations. Leave wood through barrier onto red gravel track to cross roads.

❻ **TL** onto stony farm track (the short cut joins R here) which goes uphill and through Carr House Farm. Stay on the track for another 400 metres until the 'Bridleway' Sign (R).

❼ **TR** (SO Route 11 see page 43) onto the disused railway line. Follow the very straight track back into Hetton Lyons Park. Pass pond (L) and cross tarmac path keeping on the gravel track. Continue uphill to join the main track round the park. **TR** and follow this back to the car park and the finish.

41

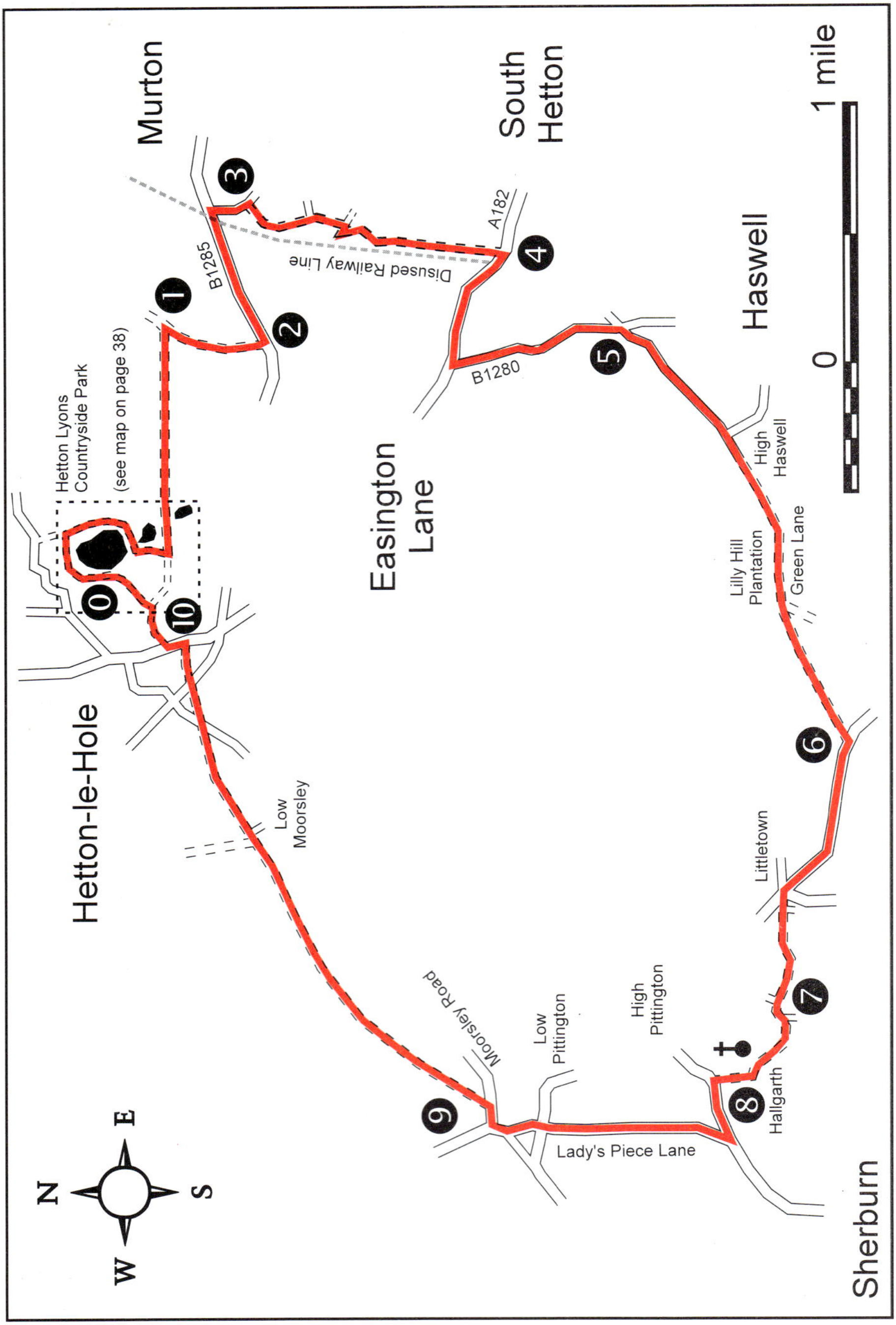
Murton
South Hetton
Haswell
Easington Lane
Hetton-le-Hole
Sherburn
Hetton Lyons Countryside Park
(see map on page 38)
B1285
A182
Disused Railway Line
B1280
High Haswell
Lilly Hill Plantation
Green Lane
Littletown
Low Moorsley
Moorsley Road
Low Pittington
High Pittington
Hallgarth
Lady's Piece Lane
0
1 mile
N
E
S
W
0
1
2
3
4
5
6
7
8
9
10

11. Et en le Haut

Hetton Lyons Circuit 3 via Easington Lane, Hallgarth and Low Pittington - A Ride in the 'Great North Forest'

Distance: 13.1 miles (21.0 Km.)

Level: Medium/Hard

Maps: Ordnance Survey Pathfinder 572 Durham

Facilities: Several pubs on route

Parking: Hetton Lyons Park, off Downs Pit Lane Hetton-le-Hole

Introduction

In researching this book I became fascinated by some of the place names I encountered on route. Many of them go back to Anglo-Saxon times. A few show Roman and French influences. The name Hetton is first recorded in 1180 as 'Heppedun' meaning a hill where rose hips grew and '-le-Hole' is the place at the foot of this hill. Murton derives its name from 'mor-tun' Old English for a fen farm. Sherburn was called 'Scireburne' in 1170, meaning a bright, pure stream.

Sometimes you can feel the presence of those distant peoples. Their settlements were named after people, tribes or the landscape, plants and animals they found nearby. As you ride this route and others in the book try to imagine a field on the bend of a river frequented by finches (Finchale); a wooden cross built on a hill (Trimdon); the valley of the wild cats (Cassop) and a cliff haunted by a spectre (Shincliffe).

Route Description

O Leave the car park and follow the tarmac path round Lyons Lake (R). At the bottom bear **L** uphill and pass Blossom Pond (L). At the top, where the main path continues **TL** onto gravel track. At fork continue past Stephenson Lake (R) and follow the very straight disused mineral line to leave the country park through barriers.

1 Continue over crossroads of tracks and under power lines. The track finishes up to a barrier and a T junction. (TL Route 10, see page 41) **TR** and follow this track to a T junction with the B1285.

2 **TL** and follow the road (there is a wide footpath if you want) down then up to the edge of Murton. Cross the disused railway on a level crossing and just past the first house (L) **TR** signposted 'Bridleway'.

3 Go past works to new bungalow (R) and fork **R** downhill and then up grassy lane. Follow this narrow track along field edges finishing across field, through hedge to a T junction. **TR** and follow track round **L** with disused railway line (R). The track continues across derelict land, part of the former South Hetton pit, past allotments (L) and finishes uphill to the 'Station Hotel' public house (L).

4 **TR** onto the A182 for ½ mile then **TL**, just before power lines, onto the B1280 to Haswell.

5 After another ¾ mile **TR** uphill onto single track road. It is a steady climb up here with a steep finish to High Haswell, but you are rewarded by excellent views of Tyneside and Wearside (R) from the top. Continue past houses and, at the end of the tarmac road, go through barrier onto wide track 'Green Lane'. There is a good ride downhill past Lily Hill Plantation (R) to a fork where you bear **R** uphill following track through gate and on to road.

43

44

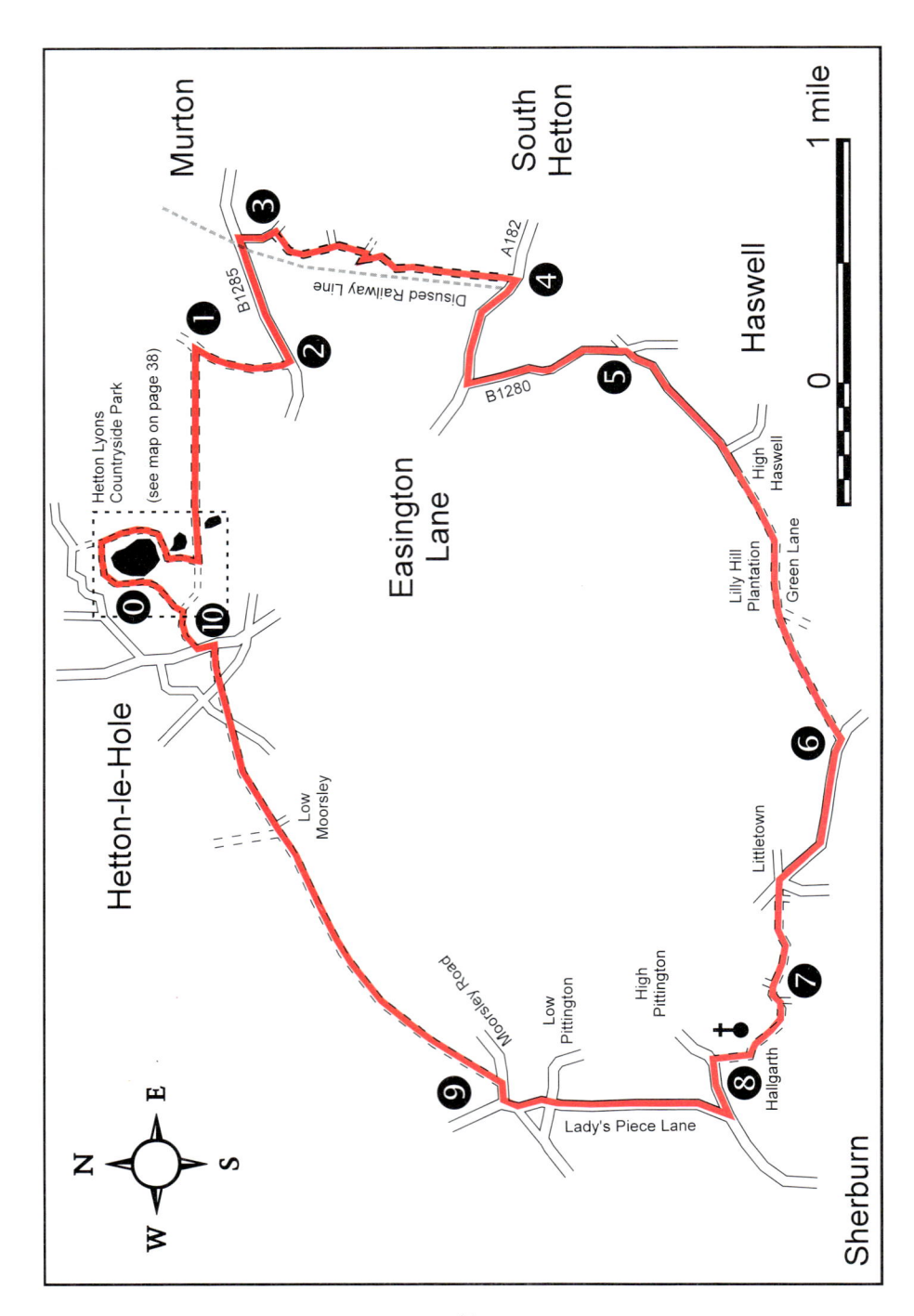

❻ **TR** and follow road to 'Duke of York' public house (R) at Littletown. Just past here is a crossroads with main road. Go over the junction onto the narrow road opposite and then through the gate at the end onto a wide grassy track down field. There is a great view of Durham with the top of the cathedral tower clearly visible ahead. Go through the gate at the bottom and onto a track that leads to the white painted Littletown Farm.

❼ Go through farm and little gate ahead onto a path that follows the field edge (L) round and over Coalford Beck on a little bridge. Continue uphill past graveyard to church gates (R).

❽ Join road bearing **L** then **R** past hall (L) to T junction with 'Hallgarth Manor Hotel & Restaurant' (R). **TL**, continue to T junction and **TR** onto 'Lady's Piece Lane'. Continue to the staggered junction and pass the 'Blacksmith's Arms' (R). Pass turning (L) and then **TR** onto 'Moorsley Road' (Route 12 joins here, see page 47).

❾ Just past the first house **TL** over barrier onto a narrow track. You will be following this old mineral line for 2¼ miles all the way back into Hetton-le-Hole. Continue on this track until you go under a bridge and onto a tarmac path. Go through barriers, crossing two roads until you come to the main road through Hetton.

❿ **TL** down the main street to 'Hetton Social Club' (R). **TR** past the club, through a barrier onto a red tarmac path that passes car park (L) and takes you, through barriers, into Lyons Park. Follow the track uphill to a T junction and **TL** onto a gravel track. At the end **TR** up a short stony hill to join the main track round the park. **TL** and follow this round to the car park and the finish.

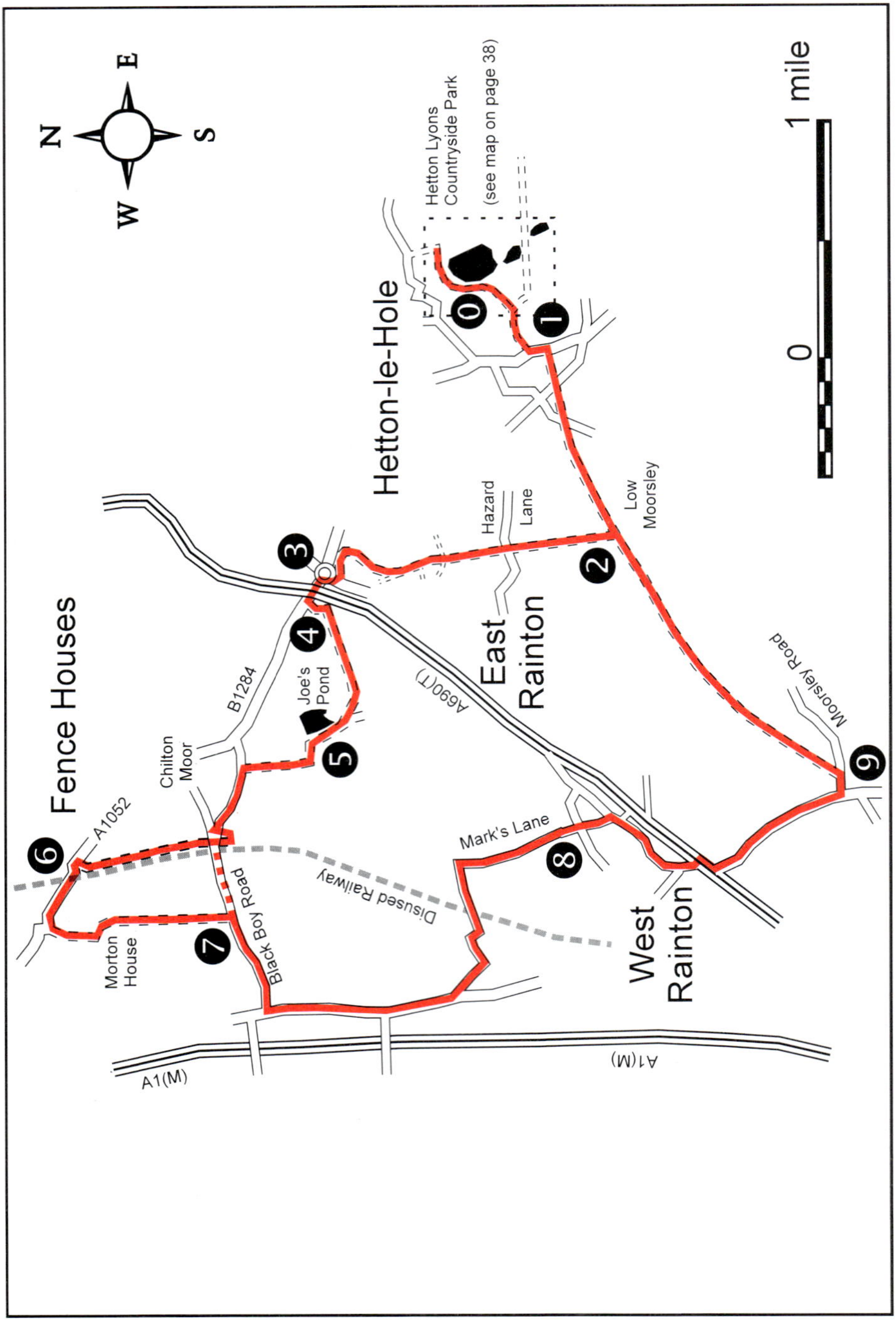
N
E
S
W
Fence Houses
Hetton-le-Hole
East Rainton
West Rainton
Hetton Lyons Countryside Park
(see map on page 38)
Hazard Lane
Low Moorsley
Moorsley Road
Mark's Lane
Black Boy Road
Disused Railway
Joe's Pond
Chilton Moor
Morton House
B1284
A1052
A690(T)
A1(M)
A1(M)
0
1 mile
0
1
2
3
4
5
6
7
8
9

12. The Means of Production

Hetton Lyons Circuit 4 via Fence Houses & West Rainton -
A Ride in the 'Great North Forest'

Distance: 13.7 miles (22.0 Km.)

Level: Medium

Maps: Ordnance Survey Pathfinder 572 Durham,

Facilities: Pubs and shops on route

Parking: Hetton Lyons Park, off Downs Pit Lane Hetton-le-Hole

Introduction

It is sometimes hard to believe that many of the areas you are cycling through were once part of the industrial heartland, not just of Britain, but of the world. At least half of this ride is on old mineral lines and it passes the former sites of nearly a dozen collieries.

Joe's Pond is a good example of changing times. It was dug in the 19th century to provide clay for making bricks. Early this century it found a new industrial use, supplying water for the engines at the nearby Nicholson's Pit. When this land was taken over by the National Coal Board in the 1950s, the pond was leased by Joe Wilson a pit sawyer. He stocked it with plants and fish, and built islands for birds to nest.

Joe's Pond became a Durham Wildlife Trust Nature Reserve in 1970. It has been gradually improved by careful management ever since. It is now nationally recognised as a Site of Special Scientific Interest.

Route Description

0 Leave the car park and **TR** to follow path round edge of lake (L). Bear **R** at bottom, uphill past allotments (R). Take next **TR** down stony bank. Almost immediately **TL** and at T junction **TR** to pass football field (L). Go through barriers and follow the red tarmac path past car park (R) up to the main road by 'Hetton Social Club'.

1 **TL** along the main street for a short distance. Just past 'Station Avenue' (L) **TR** through barrier onto disused railway track. Follow this through barriers, across two roads, uphill under a bridge and out into open countryside.

2 Just before the barrier (SO Route 11, see page 43) **TR** onto a wide uphill track. Cross 'Hazard Lane' continuing on track with excellent views (R). Go over two cross roads through plantation and downhill bearing **L** at bottom along back of houses (R). The track meets a road with a roundabout (R).

3 Cross the road and follow the tarmac path round past the roundabout (R) and **TL** onto the B1284 signposted 'Fence Houses/ Chester-le-Street, Sunderland (A690)'. Go under the flyover with the A690 above.

4 Immediately after the bridge **TL** up through a gap into the hedge onto a wide gravel track. Follow this round and uphill bearing **R** at the top onto a very straight track along an old railway embankment. Finally the track goes down to a T junction where you **TR**.

5 Pass nature reserve at 'Joe's Pond' (R). Bear **L** and **R** then straight up to a T junction. **TL** and follow narrow road past 'Chilton Mews' (R). At T junction **TL** onto 'Black Boy Road'. (For a short cut you can go straight on here) Just before the railway bridge go **L** down the steps and **TR** under the bridge onto a track. Follow the disused railway lines (L) along to the A1052 at Fence Houses.

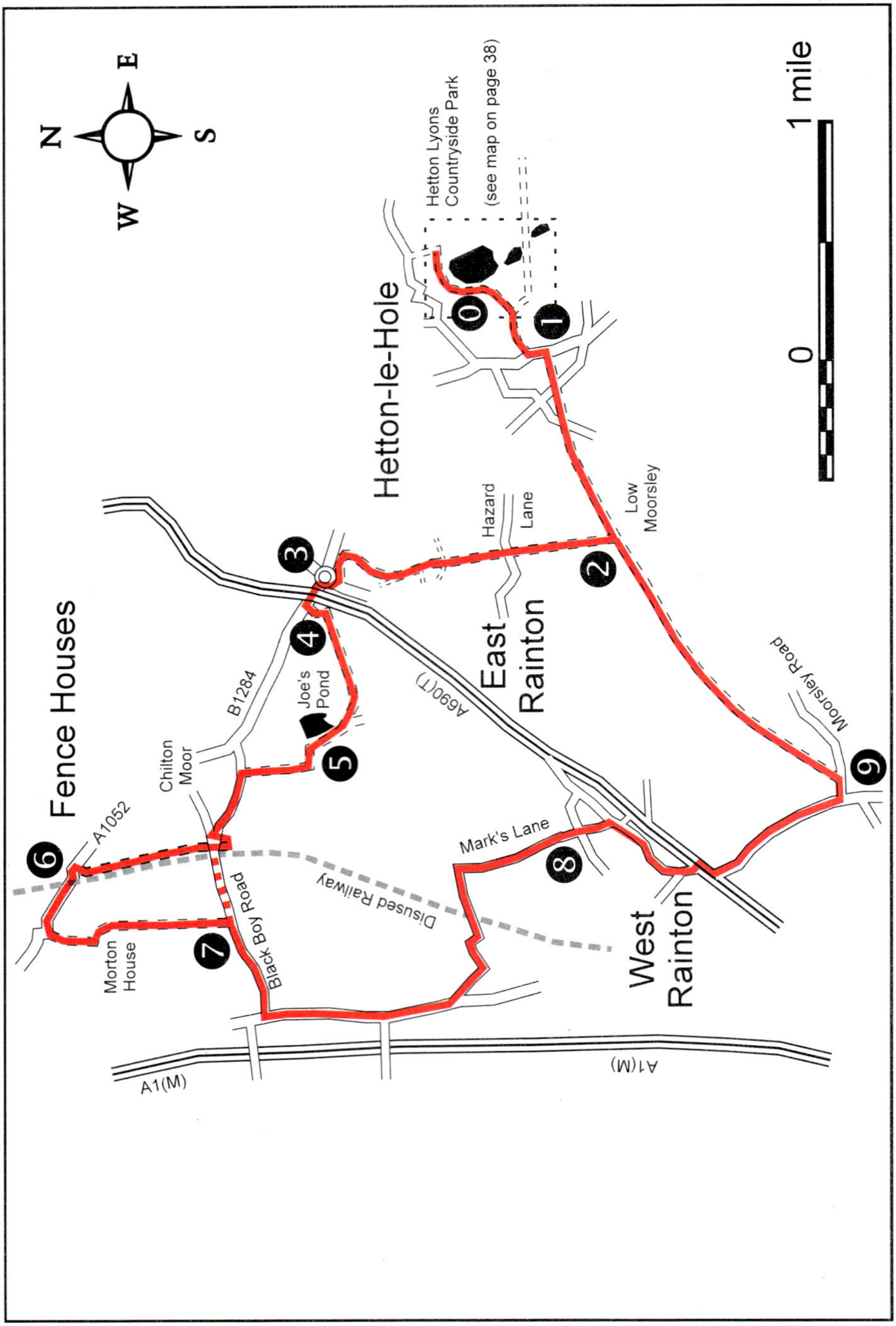
N
E
S
W
Hetton Lyons
Countryside Park
(see map on page 38)
1 mile
0
Hetton-le-Hole
Hazard
Lane
Low
Moorsley
East
Rainton
Fence Houses
B1284
Joe's
Pond
A690(T)
Chilton
Moor
A1052
Moorsley Road
Mark's Lane
Disused Railway
Black Boy Road
Morton
House
West
Rainton
A1(M)
A1(M)
0
1
2
3
4
5
6
7
8
9

❻ **TL**, go over the level crossing and down the main street. Just past the war memorial (L) **TL** signposted 'Public Bridleway Chilton Moor ¾'. Bear **L** and **R** past Morton House (R). Continue past woods (R) and farm (L) to T junction with 'Black Boy Road'. (The short-cut joins L here)

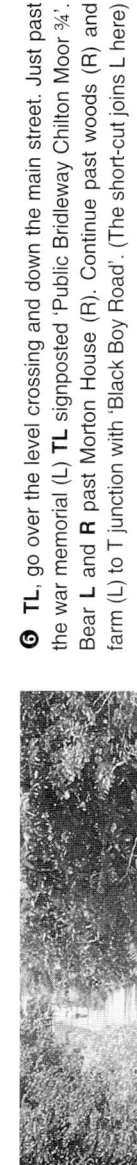

❼ **TR** along road to second T junction and **TL**. There are good views from here, including the church spire in West Rainton, where you are headed. Just past Marks Quarry **TL** onto single track road 'Mark's Lane'. This twisting lane crosses the old railway line you were following earlier, then bends **R** and goes uphill into West Rainton.

❽ Go across first road into 'Hall Lane' **TR** at next junction. Pass garage (L) and 'The Mason's Arms (R) until the road bears **L** to the A690. You will have to cross the dual carriageway here. Take great care as this road can be very busy and the vehicles are travelling very fast. **TR** down the carriageway and then **TL** signposted 'Pittington 1 Sherburn 2½'. Follow this road down for just over ½ mile then **TL**. (Route 11 joins here, see page 43)

❾ Pass white house and **TL** over barrier onto a narrow track. This joins the disused railway track that you follow all the way back into Hetton le Hole. Continue until you go under a bridge and onto a tarmac path. Go through barriers, crossing two roads until you come to the main road.

❶ **TL** down the main street to the 'Hetton Social Club' (R). **TR** past club through a barrier onto a red tarmac path that passes car park (L) and takes you, through barriers, into Lyons Park. Follow track uphill to a T junction and **TL** onto a gravel track. At the end **TR** up short stony hill to join the main track round the park. **TL** and follow this round to the car park and the finish.

49

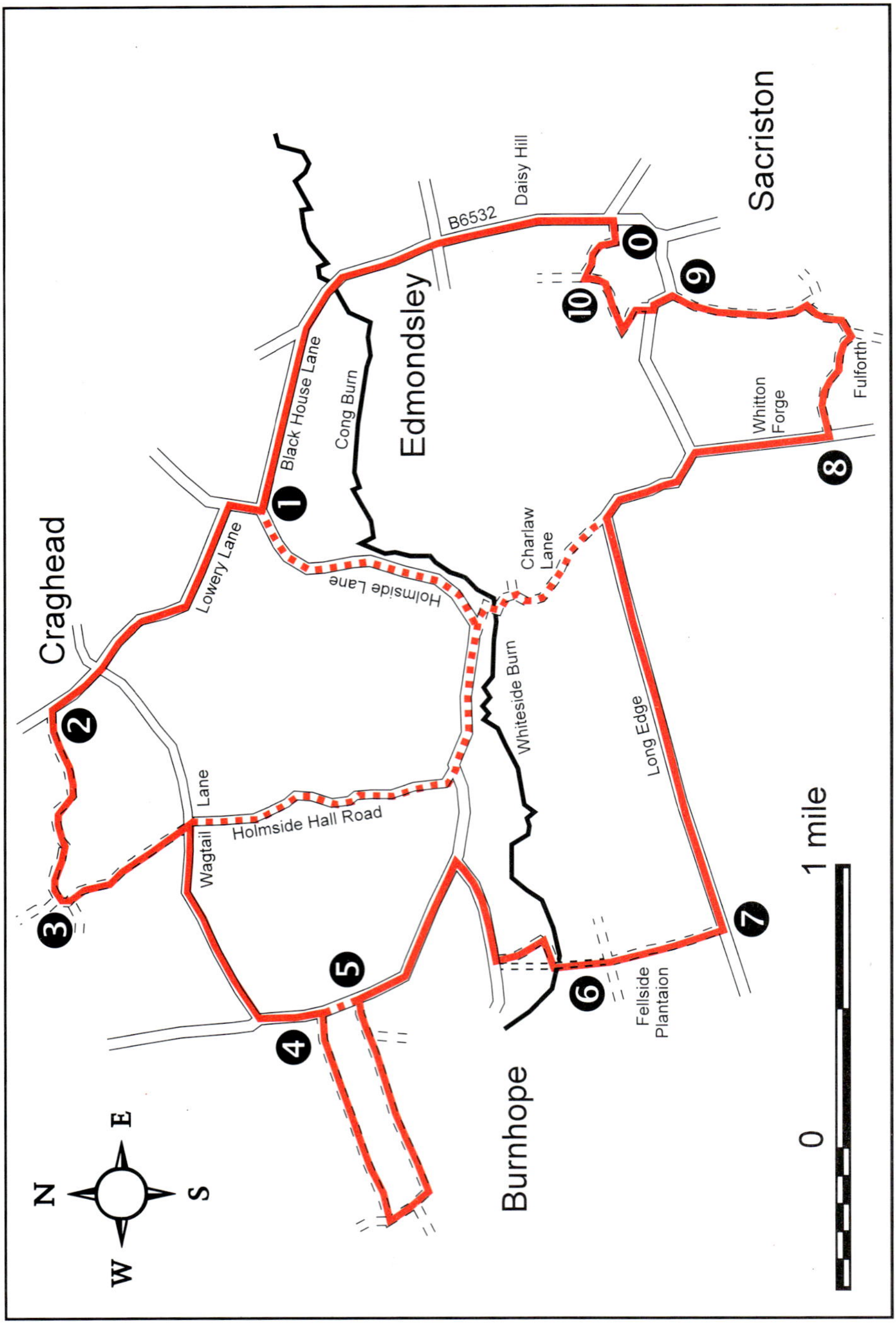

Sacriston
Daisy Hill
B6532
Edmondsley
Black House Lane
Cong Burn
Craghead
Lowery Lane
Holmside Lane
Charlaw Lane
Whitton Forge
Fulforth
Whiteside Burn
Long Edge
Lane
Wagtail
Holmside Hall Road
Fellside Plantaion
Burnhope
1 mile
0
N
E
S
W
1
2
3
4
5
6
7
8
9
10
0

13. Close to the Edge
Sacriston Circuit via Craghead and South Stanley

Distance:	13.6 miles (21.9 Km.)
Level:	Hard
Maps:	Ordnance Survey Pathfinder 572 Durham, 562 Washington & Chester-le-Street, 561 Consett and 571 Lanchester
Facilities:	Pubs & shops in Sacriston, Daisy Hill Craghead and the outskirts of Stanley.
Parking:	Turn off the B6532 road to Stanley just out of Sacriston onto 'South View' and park in large gravel area at end of road

Introduction

This is the hardest and most remote route in this guide. The section through Fellside Plantation and the alternative route down (or up) Charlaw Lane are as difficult as most experienced off road bikers could want.

My books are not written for the 'wrecking crew' types. Sometimes, when I pick up mountain biking magazines I try to visualise who they're written for. Are they seriously fit fanatics? There can't be that many! Or are they, like car magazine readers, frustrated hatchback drivers with ego lag and turbo charged imaginations? No matter which, they're probably well worth avoiding unless you want to discuss the latest titanium gizmo or how to execute the perfect abubaca, no don't ask, just get out and enjoy the scenery.

Route Description

❶ From the car park go back up 'South View' and **TL** onto the B6532. Go up through Daisy Hill then downhill and over the cross roads. Continue onto 'Black House Lane'. Pass junction (R) and continue to the cross roads with the 'Charlaw Inn' (L).

❶ **TR** signposted 'Grange Villa 1¼' and, after about 100 metres, **TL** signposted 'Craghead, Stanley B6532'. Follow this road 'Lowery Lane' uphill into Craghead. Go over cross roads and continue downhill.

❷ Just past the allotments (L) **TL** onto a bridleway. Continue on track past houses (R) bearing **R** then **L** along field edges to a small gate onto golf course. Go through gate, **TR** and follow the tree line down on a track. Cross the fairway ahead to pass club house and car park (R).

❸ By the entrance to the car park **TL** uphill on a stony track between trees. It is a long steady climb to the top and the staggered junction with 'Wagtail Lane'. (SO Alternative Route) **TR** and follow this narrow road to a T junction with main road then **TL**.

❹ After about 200 metres, just before trees (R) **TR** through white gateposts onto a bridleway. Go past deserted farm (R) onto a straight, downhill gravel track. There is a great view of upper Weardale ahead. At the bottom **TL** before pond, keep **L** at junction and go back uphill to the road.

❺ **TR** and follow the road for a fast descent. Take the next **TR** signposted 'Burnhope/Lanchester' and go up the steep hill. Just before the 'Burnhope' sign **TL** through stone gateposts onto a wide grassy bridleway. Follow this down bearing **R** at the bottom to a T junction and **TL**. Follow the narrow track uphill and through a small gate.

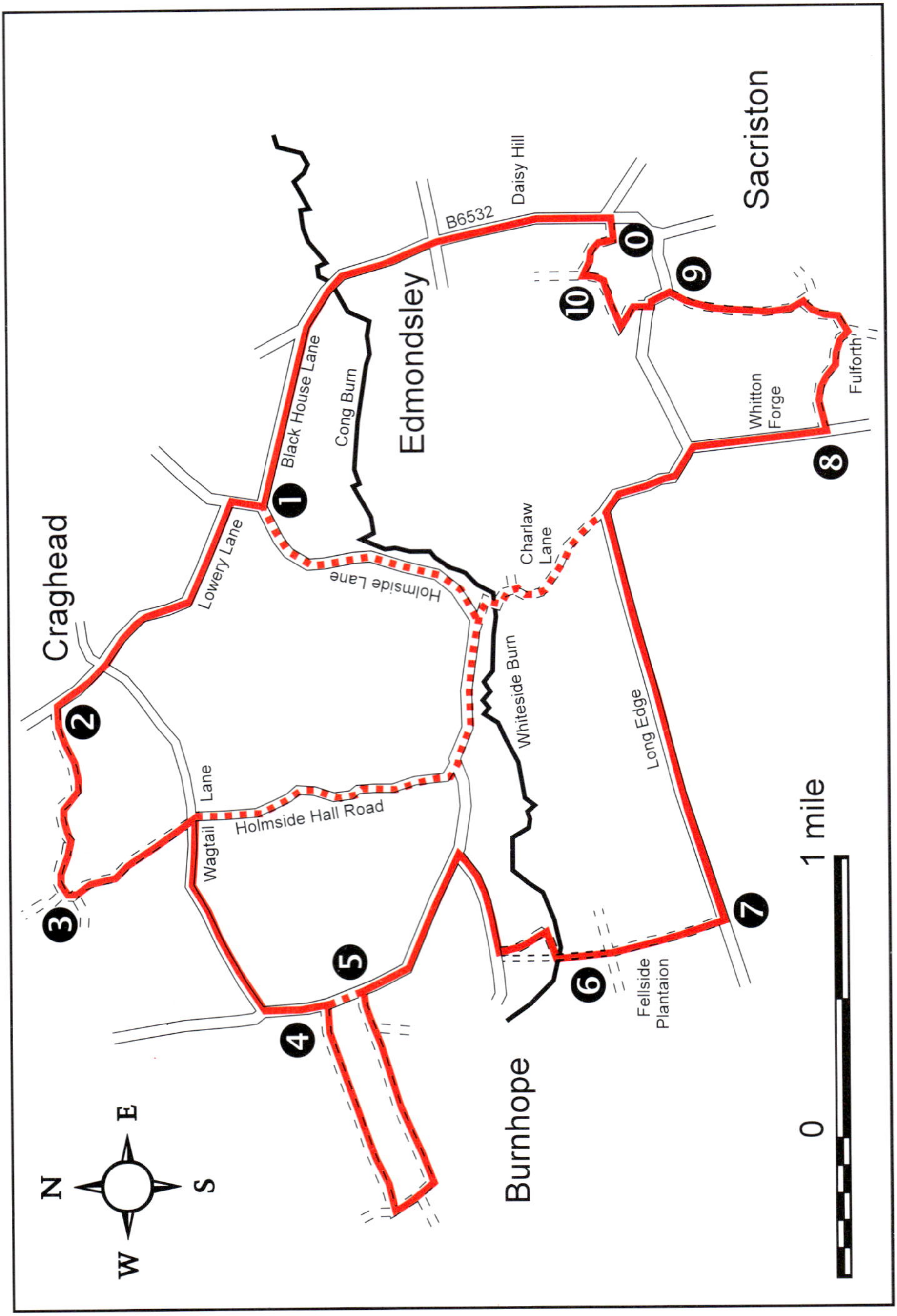

Craghead
Edmondsley
Sacriston
Burnhope
B6532
Daisy Hill
Black House Lane
Cong Burn
Lowery Lane
Holmside Lane
Charlaw Lane
Whiteside Burn
Long Edge
Whitton Forge
Fulforth
Wagtail Lane
Holmside Hall Road
Fellside Plantaion
0
1
2
3
4
5
6
7
8
9
10
N
E
S
W
0
1 mile

❻ Cross lane, go through second gate into Fellside Plantation. The way here is very cut up and indistinct. You may have to push. As you leave the forest the track becomes easier. Follow this to T junction with road 'Long Edge'.

❼ **TL** and continue on this undulating road to the radio mast where there is a panoramic view south and east. (TL Alternative Route). **TR** downhill past turning (L) and white painted farm 'Whitton Forge' (L).

❽ **TL** onto public bridleway. Pass white painted farmhouse (R) to second farm at Fulforth. Fork **L** downhill here onto a track that bears round **L**. At T junction of paths **TL** and follow path up to tarmac lane and past car breakers yard (L).

❾ At road **TL**, pass buildings and **TR** onto public bridleway. Follow this up through woods bearing **R** at top. This path follows a steep valley edge (R). Finally it goes downhill to a fork. **TR** back on yourself down to a barrier.

❿ Cross the barrier to a gravel track that bears **R** over an open area. Bear **L** over a bridge, follow the track through an S bend uphill across a barrier to the finish.

Alternative Route

From Long Edge go through metal barrier and down 'Charlaw Lane'. The track becomes steep, rutted and very muddy in winter. Finally the track bears **R** and, just before the gate **TL** very steeply downhill. It is quite hairy down here and not for the faint hearted. At the bottom cross Whiteside Burn on a small bridge and bear **L** very steeply uphill. At the top follow the field edge (L) to a small gate and road.

Here you can **TR** and follow 'Holmside Lane' back to the 'Charlaw Inn'. Alternatively you can **TL** and follow the road to the terrace of houses where you **TR** onto 'Holmside Hall Road'. Continue uphill to the cross roads with Wagtail Lane where you rejoin the main route.

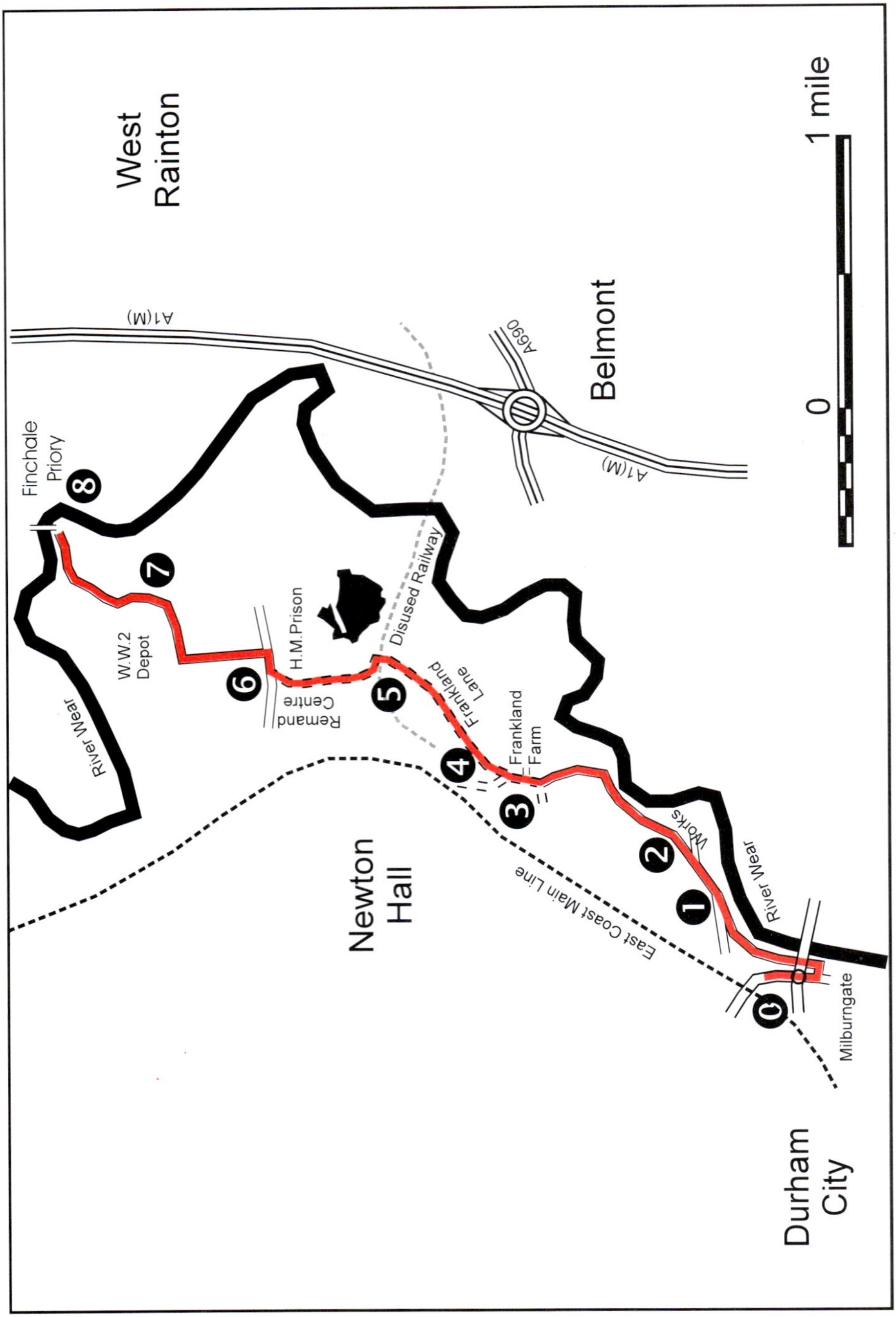
West Rainton
Belmont
Newton Hall
Durham City
A1(M)
A1(M)
A690
Finchale Priory
8
7
W.W.2 Depot
H.M.Prison
Disused Railway
6
Remand Centre
5
Frankland Lane
Frankland Farm
4
3
Works
2
1
River Wear
River Wear
East Coast Main Line
0
Milburngate
0
1 mile

14. On Holiday?
Durham City to Finchale Priory via Brasside

Distance:	4.5 miles (7.2 Km.)
Level:	Medium
Maps:	Ordnance Survey Pathfinder 572 Durham
Facilities:	Lots in Durham, shop and toilets at Finchale Priory
Parking:	Several car parks in Durham. The suggested start is at Milburngate.

Introduction

If you've done all the easy rides and want a more challenging route, this is an excellent one to start with. The terrain is varied with a couple of steep but short hills. Go on a summer's day, take some food and enjoy a picnic by Finchale Priory.

In order to get there you must pass between the bleak walls of Frankland Prison and the barbed wire fencing of Low Newton Remand Centre. Don't let anyone tell you it's an easy life inside these places. We all need freedom to survive and flourish and to be deprived of this, even by your own misdemeanours, is a punishment to anyone.

The beautiful ruins of the Priory date from the 13th century when it was apparently used as a holiday retreat for the Benedictine monks of Durham. This route may well be the same one followed by the monks as they left the city to enjoy a break by the impressively wooded banks of the River Wear.

Description

❶ Leave the car park and head into the centre of Durham going straight across the roundabout into 'Milburngate'. **TL** signposted 'Riverside' and go under the building.

❶ Continue on the road alongside the River Wear (R) past a footpath (L).

❷ Pass 'Barkers Haugh Treatment Works' (R) where the road narrows to a single track and emerges into open fields. The road finishes uphill to Frankland Farm.

❸ Go straight on past the farm (R) onto a wide gravelly bridleway.

❹ Where the main track goes L continue straight onto a narrow muddy bridleway 'Frankland Lane', which goes uphill through woods.

❺ The path crosses a disused railway line just past Dovecote Farm Boarding Kennels. Bear **L** here, but not onto the railway line. Follow the wide track round **R** and past the walls of HM Prison Frankland (R).

❻ At the T junction **TR** then almost immediately **TL** signposted 'Finchale Priory'

❼ Follow this road past an old World War II ammunition depot (L).

❽ Finish down a steep hill to the impressively set Finchale Priory. After your visit simply return to Durham the way you came.

55

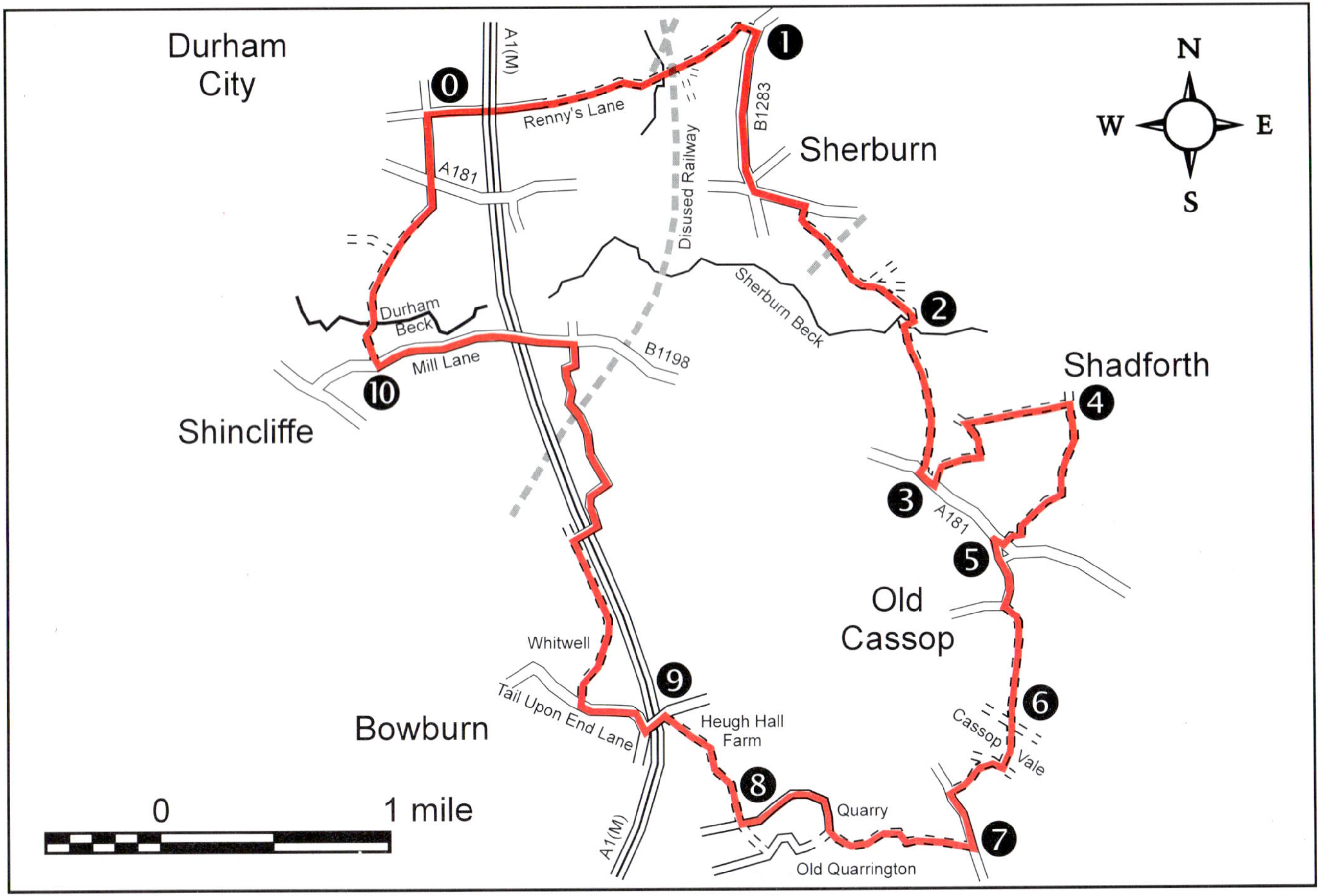

Durham
City
Shincliffe
Sherburn
Shadforth
Old
Cassop
Bowburn
N
W
E
S
0
1
2
3
4
5
6
7
8
9
10
A1(M)
Renny's Lane
A181
B1283
Disused Railway
Sherburn Beck
Durham
Beck
Mill Lane
B1198
Whitwell
Tail Upon End Lane
Heugh Hall
Farm
Cassop
Vale
Quarry
Old Quarrington
A1(M)
A181
0
1 mile

15. Turning Points

South East Durham Circuit via Sherburn, Cassop and Bowburn

Distance: 13.3 miles (21.3 Km.)

Level: Very Hard

Maps: Ordnance Survey Pathfinder 572 Durham & 581 Spennymoor & Coxoe

Facilities: Several pubs and garages on route

Parking: On street parking at Renny's Lane

Introduction

Sometimes little coincidences or contradictions come along that catch us unawares and make us think. Some seek explanations in the astrological, mystical or mythical. Perhaps a guide book is just another way that we seek to impose order on the random.

This was the first ride that I rode when I started researching this guide and the last one I tested before publishing. My companion on this ride was John Earl, a rock climber of some notoriety. John writes and edits climbing guides for Northumberland and first gave me the idea of publishing a book of cycle routes.

We rode into Sherburn soaked by a sudden downpour. By Quarrington the sky was clear and we had packed away our wet gear. The ride, the views and the weather stimulated good conversation. What has this got to do with it? Well everything and nothing can be the only answer. At least the only one I'm willing to give.

Route Description

❶ From the 'Gilesgate Moor Hotel' go down 'Renny's Lane' past industrial estate (L) and under the A1(M). Continue on tarmac path that becomes a gravel track between bushes. After about ¾ mile pass disused railway line (L) and continue downhill to a narrow bridge over Pittington Beck. Go through tunnel under the railway embankment to a fork in the path. Go straight on up the field edge (L) on an overgrown track towards the farm on the hill ahead. Join the gravel track, cross cattle grid, pass barn (R) and continue down on gravel track to the road.

❶ **TR** and follow this road to the cross roads in the centre of Sherburn. **TL** onto the B1283 and, at the edge of the village just before the allotments (R) **TR** onto a bridleway. Go past the end of 'Broadview Villas' (R) and up gravelly track to cross disused railway line. The area (L) is an old spoil heap with limy white outcrops. Take the **R** fork in the path and, after 100 metres fork **R** again. Follow this grassy track down across the field and then steeply downhill through woods.

❷ At the bottom watch out for a narrow bridge (R) over Sherburn Beck. **TR**, cross this bridge and go through gap in fence. **TL** and go uphill following the field edge (L). The path is difficult to follow here but continue to the top and go through the gate ahead. The path soon becomes a good quality bridleway that passes a disused quarry (L).

❸ At the T junction with the A181 **TL**, pass the garage and immediately **TL** uphill on narrow lane. Bear **L** past quarry then **TL** downhill at the fork. At the bottom **TR** at T junction of tracks and follow this track to Shadforth.

57

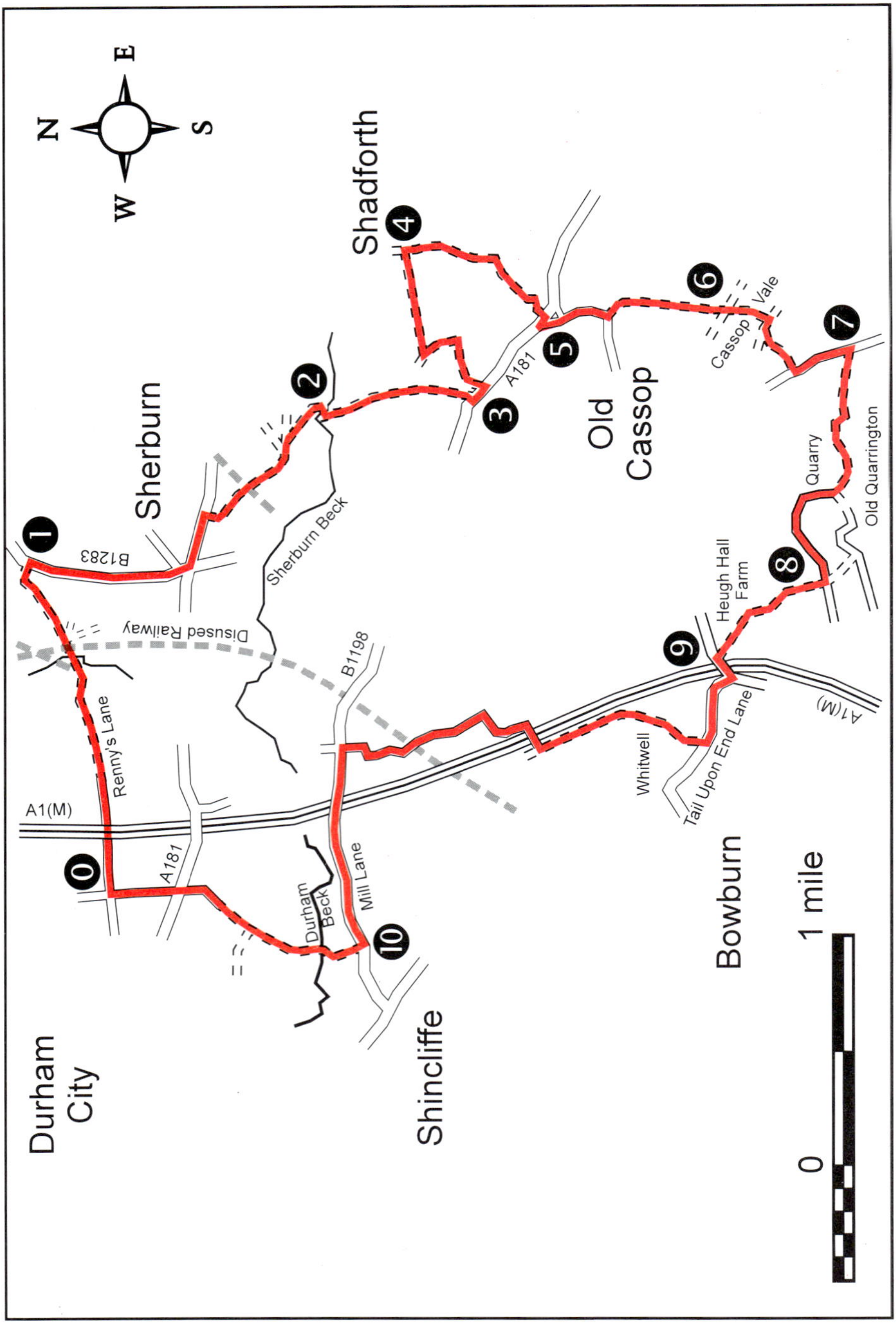
N
E
S
W
Durham City
Shincliffe
Sherburn
Shadforth
Old Cassop
Bowburn
Renny's Lane
A1(M)
A181
B1283
Disused Railway
Sherburn Beck
B1198
Durham Beck
Mill Lane
Cassop Vale
Quarry
Old Quarrington
Heugh Hall Farm
Whitwell
Tail Upon End Lane
0
1 mile
1
2
3
4
5
6
7
8
9
10

❹ At the T junction with the gravel track **TR** and pass the Georgian style mansion (L) on a bridleway up a field edge. Soon this track goes very steeply uphill. Follow field edge through gates and then bear **R** to follow fence (R) to the top where you will be rewarded by a superb view across to the distant fells of upper Weardale. Continue downhill on the deeply rutted track to a gate. Go through this into a farmyard. Pass farm buildings (R) down to a road.

❺ **TR** and almost immediately **TL** back on yourself downhill. Follow this single track road down and then uphill to Old Cassop. Where the road bears R, **TL** onto a bridleway past barn (L) and immediately fork **R** onto a stony track. Follow this track up, then through an S bend before it goes steeply downhill.

❻ This is Cassop Vale, an English Nature natural reserve. Go over cross roads of paths and onto narrow track at field edge. Go through gate and cross stream. Where the path forks **TR** then at next fork **TL** steeply uphill. For the less fit it may be a push up here to the gate at the top. The bridleway has been diverted here and is difficult to follow. Bearing **L** cross the field diagonally passing close to the white farm house ahead (R). Go through a small gate in the hedge onto a road.

❼ **TL** and follow the road until you pass an overgrown graveyard (R). **TR** onto a bridleway and go straight on ignoring the steep track down (L). The ride along this track that follows the top of an old quarry to the aptly named Old Quarrington has excellent views. You eventually join the tarmac road to the new quarry (R). Follow this road bearing round **L** over several speed humps. As it straightens out watch out for a bridleway through a set of broken down double gates (R) with a bridleway sign.

59

60

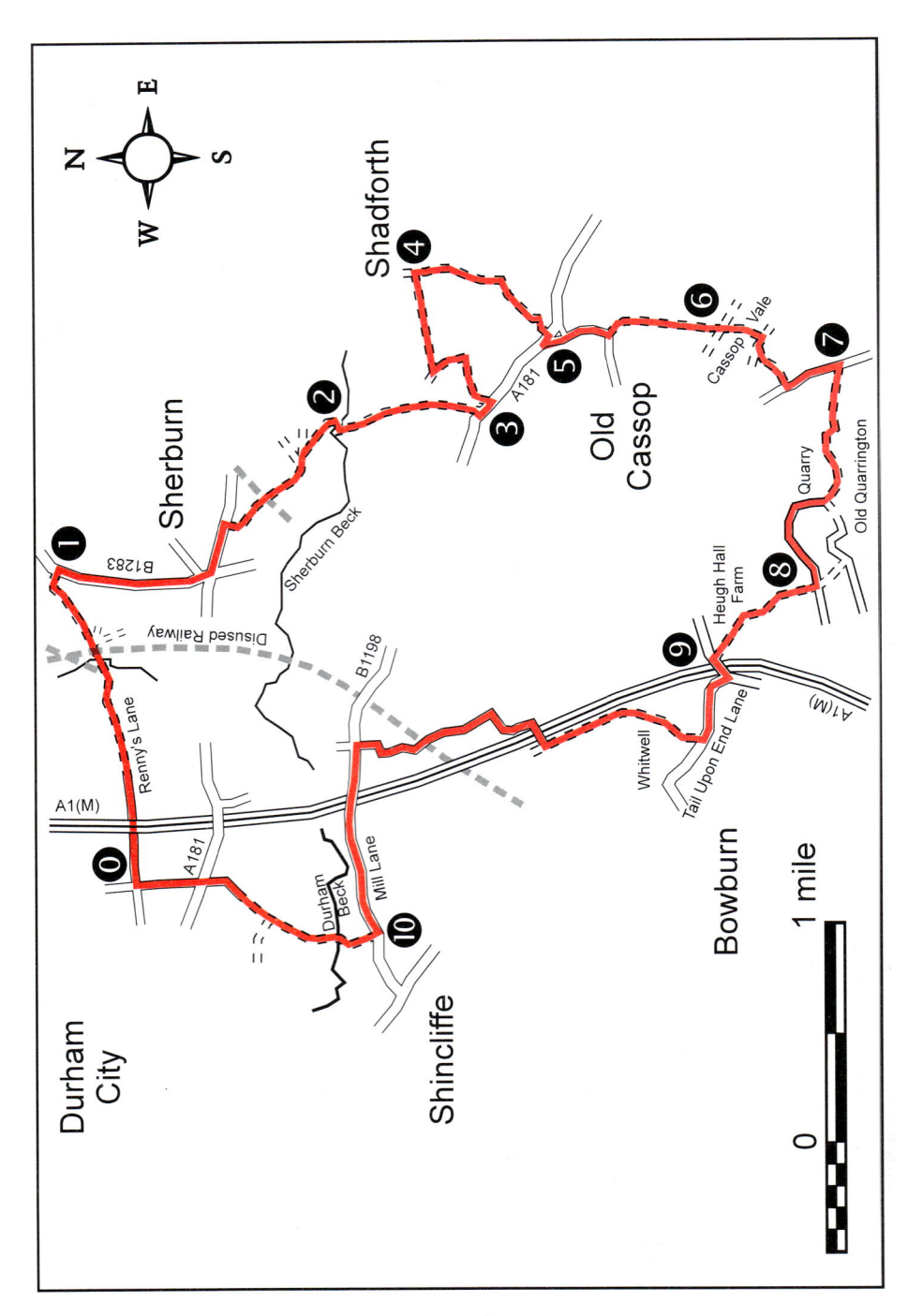

8 TR through these. Again the way is a little difficult to follow. Go across overgrown area and through two small gates. Follow hedge line (R) downhill to a gate onto a wide grassy lane. Follow this up to a gate at Heugh Hall Farm. Pass farm (R) on gravel track to main road.

9 TL, pass sign for Bowburn and cross the A1(M). **TR** signposted 'Durham 3¾' and follow this road, which has the unusual name of 'Tail upon End Lane'. As you reach the houses **TR** onto a stony lane signposted 'Whitwell School of Motoring'. (SO Route 16, see page 63) Pass farm (L) on a gravel track that goes down and then uphill to follow the A1(M) (R). At the bridge **TR** and cross the motorway. Follow the road **L** then **R**, past farm (R). **TL** and follow this road over disused railway track to a cross roads. **TL** onto the B1198 and cross the A1(M) again. Pass Shincliffe Mill Nursery (R)

10 As the main road bears R, **TR** onto a narrow tarmac lane signposted 'public bridleway'. (Route 16 joins here, see page 63) Pass water treatment works (R) where the road becomes a gravel track and cross 'Old Durham Beck'. The track now climbs steadily uphill and gives a magnificent view of Durham and the cathedral (L). At the top the track joins a road 'Bent House Lane' and if you look across R you can see most of the route you have just followed. At the cross roads go over the A181 signposted 'Renny's Lane Industrial Estate'. Go past large supermarket (L) and a little further on you will come to 'The Gilesgate Moor Hotel' (R). **TR** here to finish.

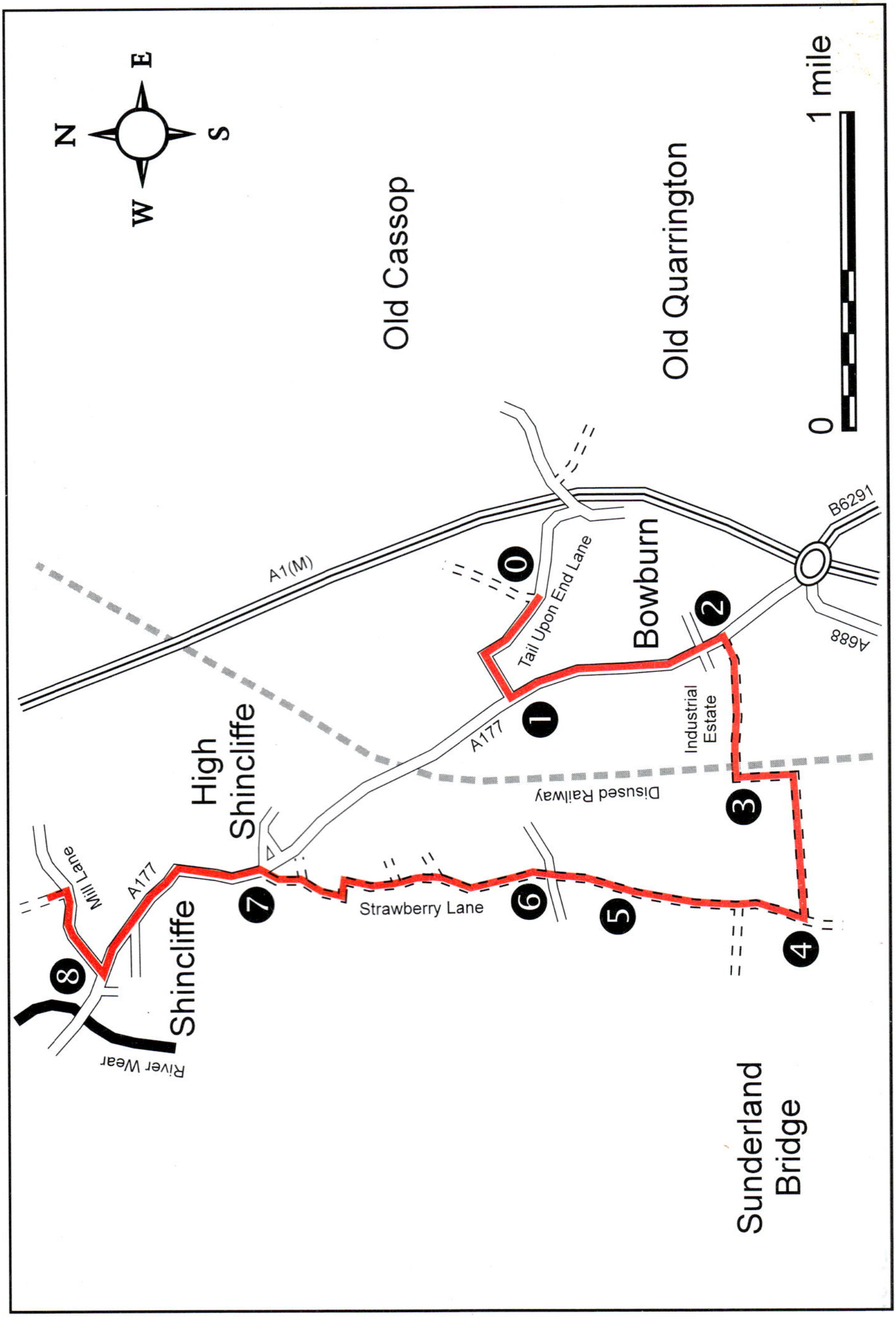
N
E
S
W
Old Cassop
Old Quarrington
0
1 mile
A1(M)
B6291
A688
Bowburn
Tail Upon End Lane
A177
Industrial Estate
Disused Railway
High Shincliffe
Strawberry Lane
Mill Lane
Shincliffe
River Wear
Sunderland Bridge
0
1
2
3
4
5
6
7
8

16. 'En passant ou a bientot'
Bowburn to Shincliffe

Distance: 4.9 miles (7.9 Km.)

Level: Easy

Maps: Ordnance Survey Pathfinder 581 Spennymoor & Coxhoe, 572 Durham

Facilities: Pubs and shops in Bowburn and Shincliffe.

Parking: Parking in Bowburn and Shincliffe

Introduction

There are several reasons for including this route. Firstly it gives a mostly off road alternative between Bowburn and Shincliffe from Route 15 (see page 57).

Secondly it means that you can ride an easy 7.5 mile circuit from Shincliffe to Bowburn by riding the end of Route 15 backwards and combining it with this route.

Finally, and perhaps most importantly, it provides an important link with the routes in my next book 'City Slicker Durham'. If you have a map you can find your own way. Turn left where I indicate in the route description (and on the map) and follow the bridleway past High Croxdale and Croxdale Hall. This will take you along the Wear and under the A167(T) to Sunderland Bridge.

From there I'm planning several new circuits to Brancepeth, Willington and Spennymoor. Who knows I might see you on the way round. Give me a wave and a 'Hello'. Even if it's not me I'm sure whoever it is will appreciate the greeting.

Route Description

O The link starts on 'Tail upon End Lane' in Bowburn where, instead of turning R on Route 15 (see page 57), you continue to the T junction with the A177.

❶ TL, pass the post office (L), cross the traffic lights and continue for a further 50 metres.

❷ At Bowburn Community Centre (L), **TR** onto a public bridleway. Follow this track until you cross a disused railway line.

❸ TL on a track that runs parallel with the railway (L). At the corner of the plantation (R) **TR** onto a very straight rutted track. Continue up to a T junction.

❹ TR onto a track that soon becomes rather narrow and very muddy in wet weather. (Just before the end of the plantation is the turning (L) through the bushes and up a field edge to Croxdale.)

❺ From the end of the plantation follow the field edge (L) down to a gate. Go up the track through a second gate to a road.

❻ Cross this road onto a public bridleway signposted 'High Shincliffe'. Follow this track, which has the lovely name of 'Strawberry Lane', past barn (L), through a gate and follow the field edge (R). At the top of the field **TL** and then **TR** to join road and continue to main road A177.

❼ This is a busy road so take care. **TL** and follow the road down into Shincliffe. Pass the 'Seven Stars' public house (L).

❽ TR at the junction signposted 'Peterlee/Hartlepool A181/A19'. This is Mill Lane which you follow for about 600 metres until you **TL** onto a bridleway to join Route 15 (see page 57)

63

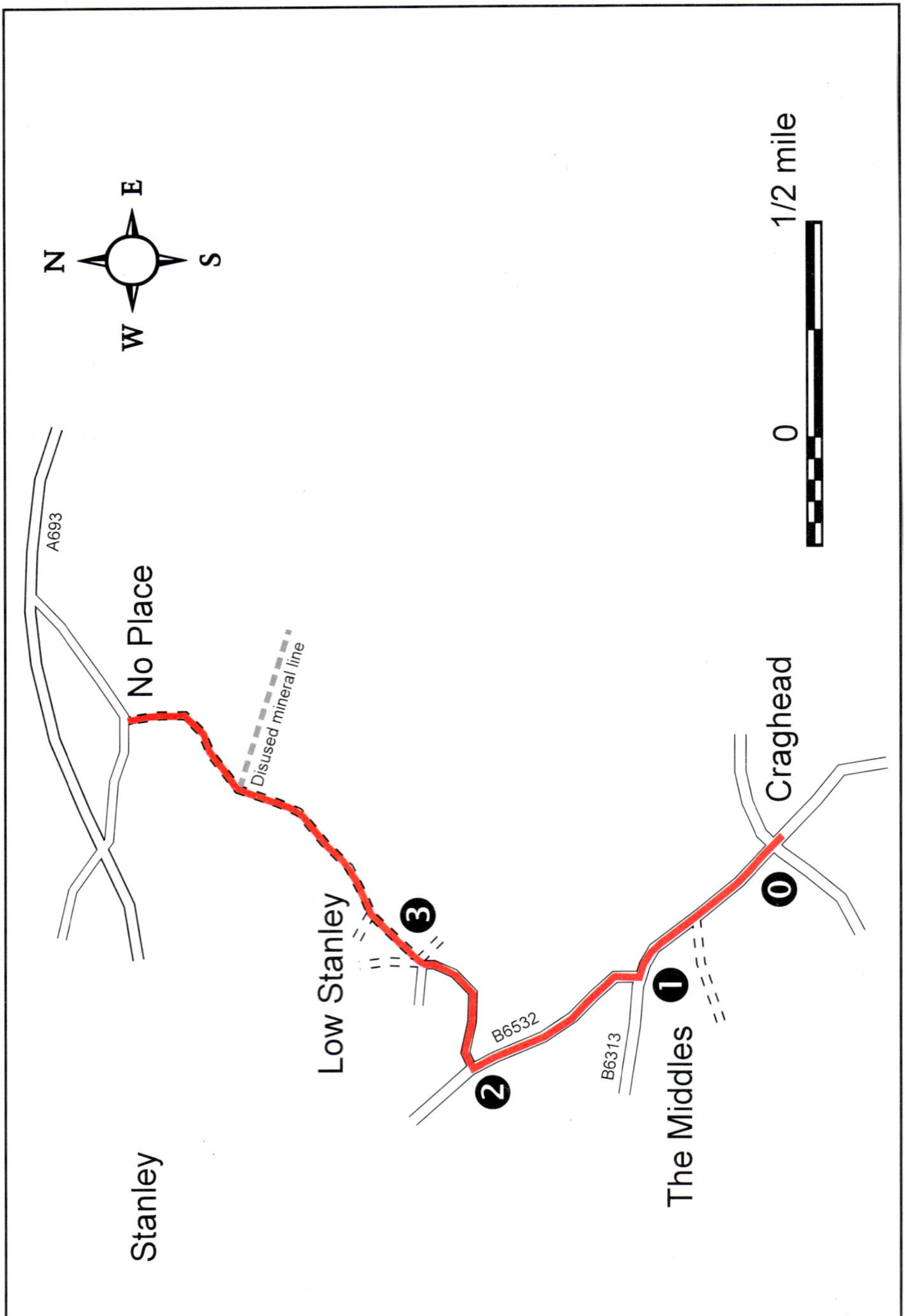

N
E
S
W
1/2 mile
0
A693
No Place
Disused mineral line
Craghead
Low Stanley
3
0
1
2
B6532
B6313
The Middles
Stanley

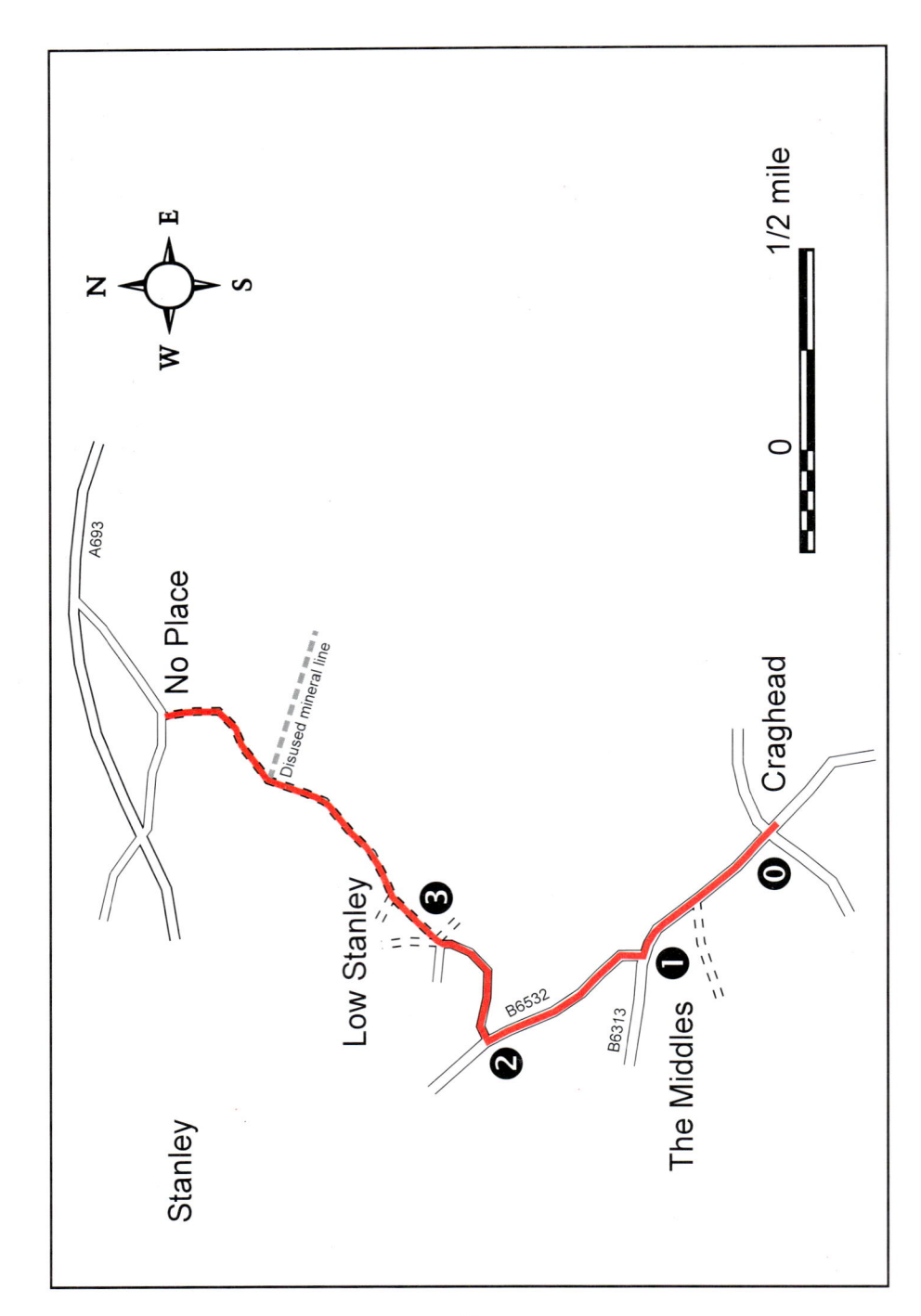

17. High Plains Drifter
to No Craghead Place and the C2C

Distance: 1.8 miles (2.9 Km.)

Level: Medium

Maps: Ordnance Survey Pathfinder 562 Washington & Chester-le-Street

Facilities: Shops and pubs on route

Introduction

In 'City Slicker Goes Upstream' (page 37) I finished a route at a dead end in Low Stanley. Well here is the continuation, not very long, not very glamorous, mostly on road but a key link in the City Slicker network.

Route Description

0 From the turning (L) for Route 13 (see page 51) continue straight on the B6313 towards Stanley.

1 **TR** signposted 'B6532 Stanley'. Continue on this road past the sign for sewage works until you reach the houses (R).

2 **TR** onto 'Cavell Place' and follow this road round past 'Pankhurst, Bronte and Nightingale Places'. The road bears **L** with fields (R). Continue to corner where the road goes L.

3 At this point there are three tracks leading away **R**. Take the middle track and go uphill under power lines. This is a footpath for the first 200 metres so you should dismount and push. Continue on this track, which climbs steadily, before crossing the track of an old mineral line (R). After this the route drops gently downhill into No Place.